# Musui's Story

Katsu Kokichi

# Musui's Story
## The Autobiography of a Tokugawa Samurai

*Translated, with an
Introduction and Notes, by*
TERUKO CRAIG

*The University of Arizona Press / Tucson*

Publication of this book is made possible in part by a grant from the Publications Program of the National Endowment for the Humanities.

First Edition

The University of Arizona Press

Copyright © 1988
The Arizona Board of Regents
All Rights Reserved

This book was set in 11/14 Linotronic 202–Galliard.
Composition by World Composition Services, Leesburg, Virginia.
Designed by Kaelin Chappell.
⊚ This book is printed on acid-free, archival-quality paper.
Manufactured in the U.S.A.

10  09  08  07  06  05          13 12 11 10 9 8

Library of Congress Cataloging-in-Publication Data

Katsu, Kokichi, 1802–1850.
  Musui's story.

    Bibliography: p.
    1. Katsu, Kokichi, 1802–1850.  2. Samurai—Japan—
Biography.  3. Japan—Social life and customs—
1600–1868.  I. Title.
DS881.5.K285A3    1988      952'.025'0924      87-36545

Cloth ISBN-13: 978-0-8165-1035-1 —
ISBN-10: 0-8165-1035-0
Paper ISBN-13: 978-0-8165-1256-0 —
ISBN-10: 0-8165-1256-6

# CONTENTS

# ACKNOWLEDGMENTS

I would like to thank the National Endowment for the Humanities for a grant in 1983–1984; Professors Katsube Mitake and Tamai Kensuke, for their generous aid in clearing up some of the more obscure passages and practices in the text; Phyllis Birnbaum and Sarah Craig, for their careful reading of the manuscript and advice on matters of style; and my husband, Albert Craig, for all his help and constant encouragement.

# INTRODUCTION

Katsu Kokichi was a samurai of the Tokugawa period (1600–1868). He was born in 1802 and died in 1850, three years before Commodore Perry's ships first arrived in Japan. In 1843, several years after he ceded the family headship to his son, Katsu wrote an autobiography. He titled it *Musui dokugen*, which I have rendered as *Musui's Story*. "Musui," meaning "dream-besotted," was the name he took after retirement; it is slightly literary and not atypical of retirement names. "Dokugen" means monologue or "talking to oneself."

*Musui's Story* is a unique document—the autobiography of a samurai who was neither a scholar nor an administrator, and certainly not a model of feudal loyalty. It is the life account of a shogunal vassal of low rank who lived on the fringes of proper samurai society and made his way among the lower-class townsmen of Edo (now Tokyo). As a youth Katsu twice ran away from home, traveling the great trunk road between Edo and Kyoto. Unable to find official employment in his adult years, he bought and sold swords. He frequented the pleasure quarters. He brawled in the streets.

He lied and stole. Indeed, the descriptions of his encounters with thieves, beggars, priests, merchants, gamblers, confidence men, and good-hearted strangers read almost like a novel, with Katsu himself as the picaresque hero. And yet his brothers were officials of status and repute, and his only son rose to become a commander of all the shogun's armies on the eve of the Meiji Restoration.

## Family

Katsu was born the third son of the Otani, a samurai house with a rank-stipend of one hundred *koku* of rice (one *koku* is slightly less than five bushels). In 1808, at the age of six, he was adopted into the Katsu house with the understanding that he would eventually marry the Katsu daughter. Adoption was a common practice among samurai in Tokugawa Japan: it provided a living for second and third sons who would not inherit the rank-stipend from their father, and it provided a necessary male heir for families without sons, thereby perpetuating the family name and hereditary income as retainers. Katsu's own father, who by birth was the third son of a blind but rich moneylender, was himself the adopted heir of the Otani house.

I have included a genealogical chart together with a few more details regarding the Otani and Katsu families in Appendix One. Here I will simply introduce several of the principal family members who appear in the autobiography.

Katsu's father: Otani Heizō was a minor official in the shogunate. He died when Katsu was twenty-five.

Katsu's half brother: Otani Hikoshirō was twenty-five years older than Katsu. After Heizō's retirement he was the family head and responsible for Katsu's conduct. He was a noted calligrapher and Confucian scholar and twice became a district administrator within the shogun's domain.

Katsu's other half brother: Saburōemon also served as a district administrator. He was adopted into the Matsusaka house.

Katsu's wife: Nobuko was the only child of the house into which Katsu was adopted. As her parents were dead at the time of the adoption, she and her grandmother lived in the Otani house while Katsu was growing up. At the age of seventeen Katsu married Nobuko and moved, together with the grandmother, to a separate house on the grounds of Hikoshirō's residence. Nobuko bore Katsu one son and three daughters. She is mentioned only once in the autobiography.

The Katsu grandmother: The grandmother of Nobuko is never mentioned by name. She was the tyrant of Katsu's young life. Although two generations older, she was more like a mother-in-law who never let Katsu forget that his adoptive house was, originally at least, of a more distinguished lineage than the Otani house of his birth.

Katsu's son: Rintarō attained fame after his father's death. He is known to history as Katsu Kaishū. In his memoirs he mentions his father only in passing.

Rank

The reader of Katsu's work may be puzzled by the repeated protestations of his honorable status as a bannerman of the shogun and the manifest indications of his lowly estate and borderline poverty. A consideration of the ranks and perquisites of samurai retainers may help explain Katsu's position in Tokugawa society.

Three classes of vassals served the Tokugawa shogun: daimyo, bannermen (*hatamoto*), and housemen (*gokenin*).

Daimyo had domains of ten thousand *koku* or more and were independent lords in their own right. By 1800 there were about 270 daimyo. Of these, house daimyo (*fudai*) staffed the highest offices of the shogunate. Bannermen had fiefs and stipends of less than ten thousand but usually more than one hundred *koku*. They were the samurai elite who served in the upper-middle-level and middle-level posts in the shogunate. There were about six thousand bannermen. Both higher-ranking bannermen and daimyo had vassals of their own. Housemen numbered about twenty thousand, held lower stipends, did not have the right of audience with the shogun, and were eligible, mostly, for low-ranking posts. Samurai as a whole made up about 6 percent of Japan's population.

As is suggested by Katsu's own story, these categories were not always as distinct as they might appear. First, the Otani family, as we noted, had a stipend of one hundred *koku*. This put it on the border between bannermen and housemen. Throughout his life Katsu claimed to have been born a bannerman. Given the official posts attained by his half brothers, this may have been so. But little is known of the Otani antecedents. Second, the lineage of the Katsu house was undeniably distinguished. Generations of its male heirs were listed in the official compendium of samurai genealogies. Even Katsu's adoptive father had had an audience with the shogun. But during the headship of Katsu's adoptive father, the fortunes of the house declined; its stipend fell to forty-one *koku*, and its status fell to that of *kobushin*, a category of unemployed samurai.

The simple fact of the matter was that in Tokugawa Japan there were more samurai than official and military posts. The shogunate instituted monthly, daily, and half-day shifts, but even then there were not enough jobs to go around. By as early as 1705 almost a quarter of the vassals of the shogun were jobless. The best-qualified were taken for posts appropriate to their rank, and the rest—including the young, the old, the sick, and the incompetent—were left idle. To handle its unemployed retainers, the shogunate set up two labor pools: the *yorigumi* for those with fiefs and stipends of more than three thousand *koku* and the larger *kobushingumi* for those with less.

During Katsu's lifetime, the *kobushingumi* was divided into eight subunits, each headed by a commissioner (*shihai*) and an assistant commissioner (*kumigashira*), who were assisted by four or five clerks or agents (*sewatoriatsukai*). The commissioner was responsible for the behavior of those in his charge. He made recommendations whenever government posts became vacant, and it was to his residence that *kobushin* aspirants to posts reported on the sixth, nineteenth, and twenty-fourth days of each month. On these occasions (called *aitai* or *ōtai*) they also submitted requests to marry, adopt an heir, retire, or make other changes affecting their life as retainers. The especially zealous lined up every morning at the front entrance of the commissioner's residence to see him off to work or presented themselves at the residence of the assistant commissioner on the fourteenth and the last days of each month.

A samurai fortunate enough to be recommended for a post was thoroughly investigated by shogunate inspectors. His domestic situation, his finances, his literary and military talents, and his deportment and that of his retainers were all looked into. If he passed muster, he received a summons to report to Edo Castle on a designated day. This was a joyous occasion, for a posting not only brought honor to his house but an office salary to supplement his rank-stipend. A number of *kobushin*, nevertheless, declined appointment, to avoid the high cost of office attire and of gifts due to superiors.

Many *kobushin* were never recommended. That was Katsu's lot. It is not surprising, considering that he was of a reckless disposition and illiterate until his early twenties. Katsu aspired to an official post while his father lived, but after Heizō's death in 1827, he resigned himself to the shameful condition of permanent unemployment. Katsu was not alone in this regard. Families were known to remain in the *kobushingumi* for generations. Settling in Honjo, Fukagawa, Koishikawa, and other tradesmen's districts of Edo, they supplemented their meager stipends by making toys, lanterns, and umbrellas or by working as carpenters, plasterers, and gatekeepers. Almost all were deeply in debt and had long since parted with their best kimono and swords. As one samurai said, in response to shogunate prescriptions of frugality:

> If you've got something to begin with, then you can speak of practicing frugality or simple living. But if you haven't got a penny in the first place, how are you going to pare down? So rather than striving for loyalty, filial piety, military preparedness, and the like, work at a trade, for only then will you be able to serve those above and support your wife and children.

Little wonder that *kobushin* samurai were known for their loose behavior and "utter disregard of the law" (*kōgi okite o shirazu*).


Personal Finances

Another contradiction that runs through the text, and indeed throughout Katsu's life, is between his poverty and his frequently flamboyant way of life. He wrote little of the day-to-day details of his personal finances, so that the reader is left wondering how he and his growing family were fed, housed, and clothed. What Katsu took for granted and barely mentioned was that most of the family's needs were met by his hereditary stipend of forty-one *koku*. This comprised twenty-three *koku* of "fief income" and eighteen *koku* of "granary rice." Of course, like other lower-ranking and lower-middle-ranking retainers of the shogun, Katsu had no fief. "Fief income" was merely an indicator of status or a memory of the past when middle-level samurai houses had once held fiefs.

The forty-one *koku* was not the amount that Katsu actually received. Just as a daimyo domain with a "face value" of ten thousand *koku* had an actual income of about thirty-five hundred *koku*, the rest providing subsistence for the cultivators of the land, so was Katsu's actual income only about 35 percent of the forty-one *koku*. Since a bale (*hyō*) of rice was roughly 35 percent of one *koku* of rice, Katsu's real income came to forty-one bales. Of this, one-third was paid in rice and the rest in money. In Katsu's time one *koku* of rice was worth about one gold *ryō*; his actual income, then, was about fourteen bales of rice and nine and a half gold *ryō*. Although Katsu never mentions going to the shogunate granary office in Asakusa to pick up his stipend, we may assume that, like other retainers, he received it in three installments: one-fourth in the spring, one-fourth in the summer, and the rest in the winter.

A grown man was estimated to eat four and a half bales of rice a year, and a woman three-fifths of that amount. Katsu's family of five or six during the 1820s no doubt consumed all the rice they received, and a little more. The cash income of nine and a half *ryō* probably did not cover the purchase of such basic commodities as soy sauce, salt, bean paste, fish, vegetables, sake, lamp oil, charcoal, and cotton cloth. It is also likely that Katsu appropriated some of the money for his personal use. As a retainer of the shogun Katsu was allotted a plot of land and a house, but he appears to have rented them out, shogunate strictures notwithstanding. Katsu's son wrote in his own memoirs that "things got a little easier" only when he was in his thirties—after his father died in 1850. Until then, he recalled, the tatami mats were ragged, the ceiling boards long gone as firewood, and one New Year's Day, the family too poor to buy the traditional rice cakes.

It would be instructive to know how family finances were handled. When Katsu was adopted as a child into the Katsu house, was it the Katsu grandmother who held the purse strings, or was it the household head, Katsu's real father, Otani Heizō? Who disbursed the coppers for Katsu's horseback-riding lessons, for instance? And after he married and went to live on the grounds of his elder half brother, was it Katsu himself, the grandmother, or the half brother who took charge? Again, after he retired in 1838 and passed on the family headship to his still-unmarried son of fifteen, did he retain some control over the stipend? We would like to know, but we are not told.

What Katsu does reveal, what he revels in relating, are his adventures in pursuit of income beyond his stipend. Various economic tracts of the Tokugawa period tell of the humble means by which most impoverished samurai made ends meet. But menial or artisanal labor was not for Katsu. Instead, he appraised and traded swords at street fairs, did "favors" for friends, recited prayers and incantations for the credulous, lent money at high interest, and organized protection for teahouses and brothels in his neighborhood. Much of his autobiography is taken up with how he used his wits, his muscle, and his position as a marginal samurai to make his way in the lower reaches of Edo society.

Exactly how profitable his dealings were is not clear. At one point he claims to have reduced a personal debt of 350 *ryō* to 40 *ryō* in two and a half years—earning an average of more than 10 *ryō* a month. Only paragraphs later, however, he notes with self-satisfaction that he earned 3½ *ryō* in three months and spent it all on a new sword.

Because Katsu lived beyond his means, he was habitually in debt. His debts, we soon realize, were for visits to the pleasure quarters, high living, street-corner generosity, and the costs of keeping up a good front. As he wrote, "appearances had to be kept up." Accordingly, he made the rounds of his superiors dressed correctly in starched jacket and over-skirt, a pair of swords thrust in his belt, and even after he had given up all hope of official employment, he wore clothes of "imported silk and fine fabrics." At the end of his auto-biography Katsu wrote that in spite of his low stipend he had lived well and wanted for nothing. To be sure, he was trying to put a good face on his life as a samurai of no significance, but we have every reason to believe that he was telling the truth.

The Autobiographer

A final question for the reader to ponder is why Katsu decided to write an autobiography at all. In the West auto-biography is often seen as a record of spiritual struggle or as a by-product of the individualism that began in the Ren-aissance. In Japan the genre became common only during the past century under Western influence. It was not entirely absent in earlier times: the philosopher and political advisor Arai Hakuseki (1657–1725) wrote an autobiography, as did the reformer-statesman Matsudaira Sadanobu (1758–1829) and the painter and Zen master Hakuin (1685–1768). They were famous men, however, while Katsu was barely literate and the black sheep of his family.

One possible reason is that Katsu developed an unusually strong sense of self. Breaking with the accepted morality and behavioral code of his class, he moved between the world of samurai and that of urban commoners. He invented a role for himself and played it with spirit, shrewdness, and imagination. Another reason, related to the first, is that Katsu may have viewed himself fancifully as a hero in the style of the popular literature of the day. He claimed to have read histories and military tales. Some of his adventures, though, resemble more the stories in *gesaku* fiction in which roguish heroes extricate themselves from one sticky situation after another. To cite one example, Katsu intimidates the peasants on a bannerman's fief by threatening to commit ritual suicide. He calls his performance a *kyōgen*, or farce; it is clear to the reader that he has no intention of carrying out the threat and that the point of the story lies in his cleverness.

Still another explanation is that Katsu knew that he was a failure by the usual standards and felt a need to justify himself. This is brought out most clearly in the contrast between the prologue and the main narrative. In the prologue Katsu assumes a more formal tone and bids future generations of his family to read his account as a cautionary tale.

Not once did I hold office, and because of me, the house of Katsu, which had served the shogun honorably for generations, was disgraced. A more telling example [of folly] you'll never find.

Yet what comes through in the text is not regret or repentance but pride. Propriety, sobriety, and bureaucratic postings may be well and good for most samurai. But he, Katsu, had chosen a different path: he had lived life fully with adventures and personal satisfactions. "I must have been born under a lucky star," he concluded, "the way I did whatever I pleased."

The Text

*Musui dokugen*, or *Musui's Story*, was first published seri-
ally from October 1899 to May 1900, in the *Kyū bakufu*, a
journal which collected information about the last years of
the Tokugawa shogunate. It was then included in volume
9 of the *Katsu Kaishū zenshū* (Collected works of Katsu
Kaishū) (1927–1929). Both versions contained a number of
errors in transcription, and in the 1960s Professor Katsube
Mitake, then of Ochanomizu University, undertook a new
transcription of the original manuscript. To make it more
readable, Professor Katsube added punctuation and quo-
tation marks, divided the narrative into chapters and paragraphs, and where feasible, corrected Katsu's highly erratic
orthography. His transcription, together with *Heishiryū sen-
sei iji*, a collection of anecdotes that Katsu wrote about a
famed swordsman of the day, was published by Heibonsha
in 1969 as number 138 in its Tōyō bunko series. This is the
most reliable edition. Another edition, transcribed by Mr.
Kawaguchi Hiroshi, was published by Chūō kōron sha in
1984, as part of volume 32 in its Nihon no meicho series.
According to Professor Katsube, the original manuscript has
disappeared and as of this writing has not yet been located.

Katsu wrote as he spoke, in the slangy, colloquial style
of the Edo townsmen district. He refers to himself as *ore*
and to others as *aitsu*—pronouns that rank at the bottom
on the Japanese scale of politeness. He uses verb endings of
comparable roughness (*nakiotta, iioru, shirananda*). He has
little sense of verbal construction and strings together phrase
after phrase with only the vaguest of connectives. His vocab-
ulary is limited—his verbs especially—and he has little concern for consistency in facts, names, or chronology. As
comments on events he regularly uses expressions such as
"Boy, was I in a fix" (*tsumaranu zama dakke*) or "He sure

had it coming to him" (*ii kibi da to omotta yo*). Even granting that the colloquial language of Edo was an appropriate vehicle for the bluff and bluster that were seen as typical of the true son of Edo, Katsu seems to have used it to excess. These same linguistic idiosyncracies, one should add, give the autobiography its freshness, vigor, and air of complete candor. The slang of a particular time and nation does not translate well into that of another, however, and so to preserve the flavor of an oral narrative, I have translated freely, using straightforward and simple contemporary English.

## Technical Notes

In the translation, though not in my introduction, I have left ages in the Japanese count, by which a child is one on the day of his birth and two on the next New Year's Day. By this reckoning a child born on New Year's Day becomes two a year later, and a child born on the last day of the year becomes two the next day.

For dates I have followed the solar-lunar calendar in use when Katsu was alive. This is most convenient for phrases such as "On the seventh day of the first month, when government offices traditionally opened." For major events of Katsu's life I have included in footnotes both the Japanese date and its closest Western calendrical equivalent.

Male Japanese in the Tokugawa period commonly used many names—one as a child, another as an adult, another if adopted, another as a pen name, and still another in retirement. Since this practice makes it difficult to identify persons in the narrative, I have standardized the various names, using the most common form. As in present-day Japanese usage family names come first.

Money in Katsu's time was complex. Domains issued paper money that circulated primarily within the domain.

Gold, silver, and copper coins were minted by the shogunate, but unminted silver also circulated. Furthermore, as the result of depreciation of the specie in coins, even coins of the same denomination often differed in value. Money changers were required to keep the system working. Gold was more widely used in eastern Japan, including Edo, and silver in the west. For the sake of intelligibility I have converted the complexity of the original to copper pennies or gold *ryō*, the units appearing most frequently in the text (see also Appendix Two).

# Musui's Story

Be patient, large of heart, and chaste,
Ever conscientious in fulfilling your duties.


Follow the path of learning,
Even though life is as fleeting as the dew on the
    roadside.

# Prologue

Confined to my house by the order of my superiors,
I spent the past year or so reading all manner of writ-
ings—tales of war, records of the house of Tokugawa,
and the like. In so doing, it came to my attention that
there are innumerable examples of brilliant generals
and brave warriors who disregarded the laws of Heaven.
Whether in governing their realms or in dealing with
their subordinates, and whether in times of war or of
peace, they resorted to tyranny or arbitrary laws and
fell into habits of luxury and lechery. And even if they
may have been successful for a while, they all eventually
lost their dominions. Again, instances of valorous warriors who fell short of accomplishing their aims and
came to grief for defying the teachings of the sages are
almost too numerous to count.

I realized that this was true for both China and
Japan: every one of those who had been brought to
ruin or lost their lands had been punished by Heaven
for neglecting the proprieties between sovereign and

subject, the bond of affection between parent, child, and brother, and for wallowing in greed and extravagance. All the more wondrous, then, that I have survived thus far without mishap. Indeed, I am so overwhelmed by the mercy and goodness of Heaven that I even hesitate to show my face to my fellow men.

Surely Heaven must have blessed me because even in the midst of my errant ways I helped people out, giving money unstintingly and rescuing them from difficulties. How else is one to account for my present state of comfort and ease?

My son, Rintarō, is serious and associates only with friends who are good and shuns the company of those who may have a bad influence. He studies the military arts, is devoted to me, and looks after his sisters. He is frugal and never wasteful, and never too proud to wear simple clothes or eat plain food. He sees to it that I lack for nothing. My daughters, too, have taken complete charge of the household and see to it that my wife and I suffer no hardship or inconvenience. My years of retirement have been truly comfortable and pleasant.

Supposing my children had turned out to be worthless like me—such comfort and ease as I now enjoy would have been impossible. This, too, is truly wondrous and leads me to believe that I have yet to be abandoned by the gods. So listen to me, grandchildren and great grandchildren—follow the example of my son Rintarō and act so that your descendants may prosper.

From the age of eight or nine leave all else and devote

yourself day and night to your studies and the military arts. Read as many books as you can—better that than some half-baked learning. Girls—from the age of ten learn how to arrange men's hair in proper samurai style and to fix your own hair as well. Take up sewing. From about thirteen do things for yourself and learn to read and write as well as the average person. For then, even after you are married, you will have no trouble managing your household. My eldest daughter has never had to ask others for help from the time she was fourteen. On the contrary, the rest of the family looks to her.

Boys—aim to be strong and sturdy of body. Eat simple food and work at mastering the military arts. If possible, strive to excel in at least one art. Serve your master the shogun with utmost loyalty and your parents with filial devotion. Treat your wife and children with benevolence and your servants with compassion. Be conscientious in your job; associate with friends in truth and sincerity. Be ever thrifty, eschew luxury, and wear simple clothes. Cultivate relations with those who are upright and seek their advice in following the path of righteousness. In choosing teachers, select those who are virtuous and without pretense, even if they are not of the first rank in their professions.

Do not consort with useless friends. Be discreet in your conversation. Respect your superiors. Keep things to yourself. Venerate your ancestors and take care that no sacrilege is committed. Arrive at your place of work one hour early. Study the literary and military arts as though you were cultivating a field. In your youth fill every hour with the pursuit of various branches of learning. Spare time only invites the devil to work his mischief. Avoid the so-called polite accomplishments. A moderate amount in old age is permissible, but if carried to excess, you'll turn out like me. Rather than planting shrubs in the garden, raise crops. Only then will you fully understand the lot of the peasant.

Strive to know the workings of the human heart. Ponder over your findings and keep them to yourself as guides to conduct. When instructing students in an art, treat them with sympathy and sincerity and be especially patient and painstaking with those who are not to your liking. Never show favoritism. In approaching all things with earnestness, you are following the path of Heaven and ensuring the happiness of your descendants. If you regard whatever you do as a duty, you should not find it hard to bear.

Above all, abstain from greed. Do not entertain it even in your dreams. I was guilty of this, and look what's become of me. Take me as a warning. Set aside possessions in accordance with your stipend. Should a friend or kinsman face an unexpected calamity, be generous in extending help. In arranging marriages for your children, do not make alliances with those above you in social station. As much as possible, choose from a poorer family. If one aims too high socially, one soon becomes arrogant. In hiring retainers, too, choose sons from poor families, and when they have completed their term of service, see to it that they are given appropriate status and rank.

Do not give yourself up to carnal pleasures. Watch

out for women—a moment's incaution can wreck family and home. Do not be remiss in discharging your social and moral obligations. Make peace among your friends in private.

Go about your household affairs with moderation and gentleness and you will never lose your authority as master of the house. Aspire to the path of the sages, for in adhering to their teachings in all things, you will avert grief and misfortune and be assured of a peaceful and tranquil life.

I myself have resolved to follow the path of righteousness henceforth. More than anything, devote yourself to learning and act in accordance with the teachings of the past. With a suitable amount of exertion, there is nothing one cannot achieve. In fact, you will find that once you've worked at something long enough, the rest will be easy. Never stray from the path of reason.

It is important to make something of oneself, gain honor and fame, and bring prosperity to one's family. Look at me, for instance. Forsaking reason and common sense, I wasted my time in activities unworthy of a human being. Not once did I hold office, and because of me, the house of Katsu, which had served the shogun honorably for generations, was disgraced. A more telling example you'll never find. True, I've finally come to my senses, but no amount of regret is going to do much good. I am regarded by my fellow men as a ne'er-do-well, and when I send someone over to retrieve any articles I might have lent, people say, "Why should we—when old Katsu got the goods dishonestly in the first place." The same goes for money I have lent. Some people have such a low opinion of me that they don't even have the courtesy to answer my requests. And come to think of it, they're probably right. In such cases, too, one should not bear a grudge. Just blame yourself for whatever has happened. Render an act of kindness to your sworn enemy and there will be no cause for trouble. As for myself, I'll admit I was resentful when I was put under house arrest by my commissioner, but then I thought the matter over carefully and realized that I had been the one who'd started the fire, so to speak. So now in atonement for my sins, I recite the Lotus Sutra every evening and secretly pray for the success of those I misjudged as spiting me. Perhaps because of this, my health has improved markedly of late, nothing untoward has occurred in my family—not a harsh word exchanged—and each day is passed in pleasant laughter. I find it truly curious, and it is to pass on this piece of wisdom to my descendants that I decided to take up my writing brush from time to time. Carefully bear in mind the fruits of good and evil.

With what awe and gratitude should we recall the debt we owe Lord Tokugawa Ieyasu, who suffered such tribulations during his childhood and endured long years of warfare. To him do we owe our present age of peace, the absence of all worries of thirst or hunger, and the comforts of family and home. We would also do well to remember the hardships of our ancestors. For us, their descendants, to tuck our hands in our kimono sleeves and live off the stipends we inherited, to forget the past and indulge in extravagant clothes and food, or worse yet, not even to serve in a government post, is surely to fail in loyalty to our masters and filial piety to our parents. Ponder on this.

Nowadays people do their work seated on the tatami without the least anxiety. At the very worst, someone may stumble and fall down. The least one can do is rise early, get to work, sleep at night without any cares, eat light and simple meals, forego luxuries, and pursue the path of righteousness.

Regard it as sufficient if your everyday clothes are not tattered. Regard it as sufficient if your clothes for office are not soiled. Likewise regard it as sufficient if your roof does not leak or the tatami on the floor is not worn through. Be frugal at all times, attend to household affairs, and consort with your colleagues in a manner appropriate to your station in life. Thrift is all to the good, but do not be stingy. Just remember the meaning of the two Chinese ideographs "frugal" and "miserly." In reading books, too, if your attitude is wrong, you will end up as some good-for-nothing's dictionary or bookcase. The same is true of the military arts. If you go about your training as if it's an exercise in brutish strength, your limbs will become muscle-bound and you will be about as much use as someone's sword rack. Take these words to heart.

The same rule applies to becoming a real human being. If you succumb to avarice, you may appear human on the surface, but inside you are but a cat or dog. Your first concern should be to strive for true humanity. If you do not pursue learning and the military arts with the correct attitude, you will become a cripple and misfit and might as well not study at all. Remember well how important it is to have the proper spirit.

Children and grandchildren—heed my advice. As I have said, I am altogether ignorant when it comes to writing difficult characters and have made many errors in setting down this record. Read it, nevertheless, with great thought and care.

Early Winter, The Fourteenth Year of Tenpō*
Written at Uguisudani

*1843.

# Childhood

There can't be many in the world as foolish as I am. So let me say this to my grandchildren and great grandchildren—listen to what I have to say, and may the scoundrels and fools, especially, take my story as a lesson.

I was the child of my father's concubine. She fell out of favor with him, and I was born in her family home.* I was then taken in by my father's wife—I think of her as my real mother—and put under the care of a wet nurse. I was naughty from the time I was little and made life difficult for my mother, and with my father away at his office every day, I acted up and was so headstrong that all were at their wits' end. Or so our old retainer Riheiji told me years later.

We lived in the Aburahori section of Fukagawa. In the garden there was an ornamental pond that was filled with water drawn from one of the nearby canals.

*Kyōwa 2 (1802).

During the summer, I would swim in it every day. I knew that my father returned from work around two in the afternoon, so just before he came back, I would get out of the water and amuse myself with something else, looking the picture of innocence. My father would ask Riheiji why the water in the pond was always so muddy. Old Riheiji said that he had never quite known what to say.

My mother suffered from palsy and had trouble getting around. The rest of the household was also female. I looked down on all of them and spent my days getting into one kind of mischief or another. My older brother Hikoshirō already lived in his own house and had no idea what was going on.

When I was five, I took part in a kite fight against Chōkichi, the son of a laborer in Mae-chō. Chōkichi, who was older by about three years, seized my kite, smashed it, and took away the string. I picked up a jagged rock, and grabbing hold of the collar of his kimono, hit him in the face. Blood came spurting out of his mangled lips, and Chōkichi began bawling.

My father happened to see this from over the garden fence. He sent one of his men to fetch me home. "What do you mean," he said angrily, "hurting someone's child like that? You can't be left unpunished!" He tied me to one of the posts in the veranda and whacked me on the head with a wooden clog. To this day I have a bald spot and a dent where he struck me. The razor gets caught and nicks the skin whenever I have my head shaved, and each time I'm reminded of that Chō-kichi.

My mother would put away the sweets and cakes

that people gave us. I would steal them, so she took to hiding them here and there. Sooner or later I'd find them anyway, but she could never bring herself to report it to my father. In fact, since she had been the one who'd decided to take me in, she covered up for me all the time. And as for the servants and retainers in the house, they were too much in awe of her to say a word to my father.

I grew up a real hell-raiser. One year on Boy's Day in the fifth month, sheaves of irises had been hung under the eaves as was the custom.[1] I kept stealing them so I could play a game of slap-the-iris-leaves with my friends. At first Riheiji said nothing, but by the fifth time it happened, his patience ran out.

"Enough is enough," he complained to my father.

"Look," my father replied. "Children are supposed to be full of spirit. Otherwise they become sickly and have to see the doctor. Just buy plenty of irises and keep hanging them up."

"And a lot of bother it was, too," Riheiji sighed, after he told me this story when I was sixteen or seventeen.

Old Riheiji worked for us for many years, even going all the way to Shinano Province to accompany Hiko-shirō, who had been appointed as the administrator of a shogunal district.[2] The retainers my brother took with him at the time were of non-samurai rank. They were each given money to buy samurai status when they returned to Edo five years later. Riheiji alone decided to retire and taking his share of the money, went to live with a relative. He was cheated of every penny by this man and obliged to come back to my brother's house. There, he was regarded by the other retainers as a nuisance. I felt sorry for Riheiji, and after arranging for him to become a lay priest, I sent him off on a pilgrimage around the country. That didn't last long, and I next set him up as a caretaker at the Kannōji temple in Yanaka. He died shortly after, but all this took place years later, when I was about thirty.

I was adopted by the Katsu family when I was seven.* My age was officially given as seventeen, and the hair at the front of my head was cut off accordingly.[3] As part of the adoption procedure,[4] Ishikawa Ukon-no-shōgen, the commissioner of my unit at the *kobushin-gumi*, and his assistant, Obi Daishichirō, came to the house.

"How old are you and what is your name?" Ishikawa asked.

"My name is Kokichi and I am seventeen."

Ishikawa pretended to be taken aback. "Well—for seventeen you certainly look old!" He burst out laughing.

My adoptive father's older brother, Aoki Jinbei, who served at Edo Castle as a member of the Great Guard, acted as sponsor.

Until then I had been called Kamematsu. With my adoption my name was changed to Kokichi. My adoptive parents had already died, leaving behind a daughter and her grandmother. It was decided that the two would live at my father's place in Fukagawa. I was completely ignorant of these arrangements and spent my time in play.

*Bunka 5 (1808).

I got into another fight over a kite, again with some boys from Mae-chō. There must have been twenty or thirty. I took them on alone hitting and punching, but they finally got the better of me. I was cornered on a large rock in an open field and struck over and over with bamboo poles. My hair had fallen loose all over my face, and I was sobbing. I took out my short sword* and slashed left and right. But I knew I was beaten and decided then and there to commit harakiri. I stripped to the waist and sat down on the rock. As it so happened, a rice dealer by the name of Shirokoya was standing nearby. He talked me into giving up the idea and took me home. After this, though, all the boys in the neighborhood became my followers. I was seven at the time.

Our house in Fukagawa was close to the sea and was flooded from time to time. My father received permission to move to Honjo. Until the new house was ready, we rented the residence of someone called Waka-bayashi in Surugadai, on the other side of Ōtahime Inari Shrine. The house was enormous, with an imposing garden and next to it a field at least a third of an acre. Everyone said it was haunted.

One evening—I must have been eight or so—my father called together the entire household and ordered us to tell each other ghost stories in the dark.[5] He said we were to put up a straw doll in the adjoining field, and after the last story had been told, we were to go

---

*On reaching the age of discretion, samurai boys were allowed to carry short, blunt-edged swords.

one by one and tie a piece of paper with our name to the sleeve of the doll's kimono. It was funny to see everyone so scared. I was supposed to go last and stick a polished copper coin in the center of the doll's face—just like an eye. By the time my turn came, it was past midnight and pitch black. I had to grope around for a while, but I did it, and everyone praised me.

My grandmother by adoption had been known for her mean disposition from the time she was a young girl. It was said that she drove both of my adoptive parents to an early death. She was nasty to me, too, and nagged and scolded day after day. I would lose my temper and fight back with every insult I could think of. My father overheard me one day and called me over. "So—who do you think you are, talking like that to your grandmother at your age? No telling what you'll do in the future!" He bared his dagger and came at me. His wife, Kiyo,* apologized for me in the nick of time.

The following year we moved to the new house in Kamezawa-chō, Honjo. For the first time I was settled together with my grandmother in rooms toward the front of the house. She could now scold me all she wanted, and if that wasn't bad enough, she served up the most awful meals. How I hated her!

I spent most of my time away from home and got into one scrape after another. One day my pet dog got into a vicious fight with a dog that belonged to someone in Kamezawa-chō. With me at the time were Anzai Yōjirō—he was fourteen and the leader of our gang—

*Probably the first wife of Katsu's father and the one who took Katsu in.

Kurobe Kintarō, Kurobe Kenkichi, Shinoki Daijirō, Aoki Shimenosuke, Takahama Hikosaburō, and my younger brother, Tessaku.*

The eight of us started beating up the dog's owner and his friends in front of my house. The boys from Kamezawa-chō sent for help, and pretty soon forty or fifty kids, all armed with bamboo spears, showed up from Midori-chō. We got hold of wooden swords and poles and managed to drive them away. They soon returned for another attack with several grown-ups as reinforcement. We put up a good fight, but when it became clear that we were losing, we withdrew behind the front gate of our neighbors, the Takigawa family.

Scarcely had we caught our breath when the other side, flushed with victory, began ramming the gate with a log. Desperate, we decided to use our blunt-edged swords. We flung open the gate, charged at the boys, and sent them flying away. We ran after them, waving our swords.

My younger brother—just seven but a real fighter—was ahead up in front when Benji, a tailor's son from Mae-chō, turned back and jabbed him in the chest with a bamboo spear. I rushed up to Benji and struck him in the forehead with my sword. That good-for-nothing Benji flopped on his rear and landed right in a ditch. So for good measure I gave him a few more blows on the face.

The fathers of some of the Mae-chō boys came running to the scene. What an uproar! The eight of us let out a hearty cheer. We then returned to the Takigawa

*Not in the official genealogy.

residence and congratulated one another. My father, who had been watching all this from one of the rooms flanking the front gate, was very angry. He confined me to my room and ordered me to stay out of his sight for the next thirty days. Tessaku was locked up in the storehouse for five or six days.

When I was nine, my father told me to take judo lessons with Suzuki Seibei, a relative of the Katsu family in Yokoami-chō. Suzuki served as the head of the office of procurements and was reputed to have many students, among them daimyo from provincial domains and from the great houses of Hitotsubashi and Tayasu. The classes I attended were held on the third, fifth, eighth, and tenth days of each month. I behaved myself at first but soon got into mischief. My fellow students strongly disliked me and ganged up against me all the time.

On my way to class one day I found to my great surprise that a crowd of boys from Mae-chō and their parents were lying in wait for me near the Hannoki riding ground. "Here comes that troublemaker Otani— let's beat him to a pulp!" they yelled, and flourishing bamboo spears and sticks, they quickly closed in on me. I drew my sword, slashed my way out, and clambered up the embankment of the riding ground. Just below was a muddy ditch that surrounded the shogunate lumberyard. I jumped in. I spattered my *haori* and *hakama*,* but at least I had escaped. The gatekeeper

*A *haori* is a kimono-like jacket, and a *hakama* is a divided skirt worn over a kimono. Both are worn when formal dress is required.

of the lumberyard was a friend of mine—I often went there to play—and knowing he was a brave man, I had him walk me home. Forty or fifty people were still waiting. Did we get a thrashing!

For two months I avoided that section of Kamezawa-chō. Then one day I caught Tatsu, the son of an embroidery craftsman in Kamezawa-chō, walking by our house. I ran out and struck him with my sword until one of our retainers had to come out and restrain me. He told me later that he had taken Tatsu home and explained to his parents that I was only trying to get even for what had happened near the riding ground. In any case, no one in Kamezawa-chō crossed me after that.

As I said, everyone in judo class hated me. On the day that an all-night midwinter session was to be held, we received permission from the teacher to bring food. We took a break at midnight. I had packed a lacquer box full of bean jam cakes and had been looking forward all day to this moment when we would share the food. My classmates had other plans. They got together and tied me up with an obi, hoisted me to one of the rafters, and began eating, even helping themselves to my cakes. So I pissed on their heads, spraying the food that had been spread out, and naturally, everything had to be thrown away. Served them right, too.

I was ten. In the summer I began riding lessons with Isshiki Ikujirō, a guard at the Edo Castle who lived in Kikugawa-chō in Fukagawa. Lessons were held at a riding ground at the Iyodonobashi residence of Jinbō Isosaburō, a samurai with a stipend of six thousand *koku.* I liked riding and rode around the ground day after day. After about a month I decided to go out beyond the gates, but once on the street, who did I run into but my teacher. I quickly turned into a side alley. At the next lesson he gave me a scolding. "Why, you don't even know how to ride in a saddle properly. You will desist from leaving the ground for the time being."

I switched to another teacher, Ōkubo Kanjirō, and learned how to handle a horse. My new teacher was excellent, telling me among other things to practice daily on a wooden horse. He also said I should ride on a saddled horse fifty times a month. I had the stable boy rent horses from Tōsuke, Denzō, and Ichigorō and spent all my time riding. In the end I got a horse of my own and kept it at Tōsuke's stable.

I was fascinated by fires and rushed to see one whenever I could. One day I heard a fire had broken out in Bakuro-chō and dashed over on my horse. I was scolded sharply by a courier called Imai Tatewaki and chased all the way to the residence of the Tsugaru domain in Honjo. My horse was too fast for him, though, and I was finally able to throw him off. I learned afterward that you're not supposed to go within three hundred yards of a fire.

On another occasion I borrowed a horse from Denzō and galloped full speed on the embankment of the Sumida River. For some reason a strap suddenly broke, and one stirrup fell into the river. I had to go all the way back with only the other.

When I was eleven, I became a student of Udono Jinzaemon, a swordmaster in Surugadai. I had first heard about him from my friends, who said that he was a master of the Chūya-ryū and Ittō-ryū schools of fencing and retained by one of the Tokugawa consorts. I liked the fact that Udono exclusively taught the technique for the wooden sword, and I practiced diligently. Before long I was initiated into a technique called the *sō*.[6]

The son of Ishikawa Ukon-no-shōgen, my commissioner at the *kobushingumi*, was also in my class. He knew all about me—how much my stipend was and so forth—and taunted me in front of the other students at every opportunity. "Katsu, what's your stipend? A measly forty bales of rice! Ha ha ha." Since he was the commissioner's son, I kept quiet.

He continued to make fun of me. So one day I hit him good and hard with my wooden sword, cursed him out, and left him blubbering. I received a terrible scolding from the teacher. That so-and-so now goes by the name of Ishikawa Tarōzaemon and holds the post of Captain of the Foot Soldiers. An old fogey and stupid just like a woman—he'll never amount to much.

When I was twelve, my brother Hikoshirō arranged for me to begin school.* He took me to the shogunate academy in Yushima. I began by studying the Chinese classic, the *Greater Learning*, with Hoki Minokichi and Sano Gunzaemon, officials in charge of the school dormitory. I hated studying, and every day slipped out through the fence and into the Sakura riding ground, where I spent hours riding. At most I learned to read five or six pages of the *Greater Learning*. The two

*Bunka 10 (1813).

teachers soon sent word that they didn't want me, which suited me just fine.

I did nothing but ride, and with my money all gone, I began stealing from my mother's pin money and the cash she had set aside for emergencies. My brother was away in Shinano at the time on a five-year assignment as district administrator. In his third year he came back to Edo for an audience with the shogun. When he heard that I was spending all my time and money on riding, he ordered me to give up lessons and sent a letter to my teacher giving notice. He also scolded me severely and told me to stay at home. For a while I couldn't leave the house, and what a pain that was.

The following autumn—I was thirteen—Hikoshirō returned to Shinano. I was once more free to roam and loaf about as I liked.

My grandmother was as mean as ever. She only had to see my face and she would start berating me about this or that. In desperation I went to my brother's wife for advice. She took pity on me and promised to speak to my father. One day he said to my grandmother, "Kokichi is growing up. With his low stipend, if he doesn't know how to cook, he won't be able to manage in the future. From now on, why don't you let him cook for himself?"

My grandmother took this as an excuse to do absolutely nothing for me and left me to prepare all my meals. At the same time, she kept thinking up ways to make my life as wretched as possible—I once found that she had even diluted my soy sauce with water. If anyone gave us cakes or other delicacies, she would hide them and give me none. But if she so much as sewed a kimono for me, she would announce it to the whole world, telling everyone in the same breath what an ungrateful child I was. She made me furious. Worse still, I couldn't complain to my father, since he would only rebuke me. I can't remember ever having been so miserable.

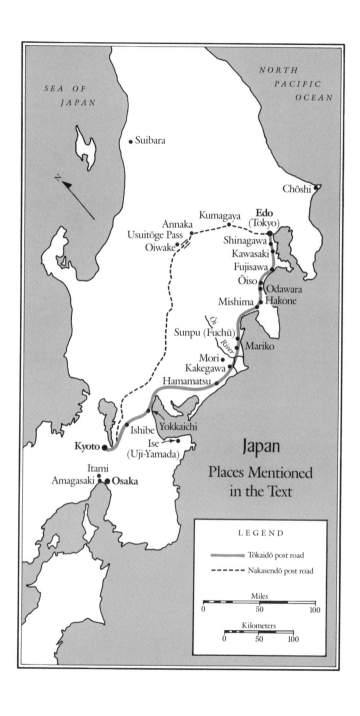

N

• Suibara

Chōshi •

Kumagaya •   **Edo**
Annaka •              (Tokyo)
Usuitōge Pass •          Shinagawa
Oiwake •              Kawasaki
                      Fujisawa
                    Ōiso •
                          Odawara
Mishima •          Hakone
            Ōi
Sunpu (Fuchū) •  River
                      Mariko
          Mori •
Kakegawa •
Hamamatsu •

Ishibe •  Yokkaichi •
**Kyoto** •  Ise •
        (Uji-Yamada)
Itami •
Amagasaki • • **Osaka**

Japan

Places Mentioned
in the Text

LEGEND

━━━  Tōkaidō post road
- - -  Nakasendō post road

Miles
0       50       100

Kilometers
0       50     100

# I Run Away

I was fourteen.* I made up my mind to run away to the Kyoto area and stay there for the rest of my life. After all, I thought, no matter what a man puts his hand to, he'll always be able to eat.

On the twenty-eighth day of the fifth month, I put on a pair of trousers over my kimono and set off. I didn't know a thing about the world, and as for money, I had only the seven or eight gold *ryō* I had stolen and tucked in the band I wrapped around my stomach. Asking directions along the way, I got as far as Shinagawa. I was lonely and frightened, but I pressed on and stayed the night at an inn in Fujisawa.

The next morning I woke up early and walked about aimlessly, wondering what to do. Two tradesmen caught up with me. "Where are you heading?" they asked.

"Nowhere in particular," I said. "Maybe someplace near Kyoto."

*Bunka 12 (1815).

"Come along with us—we're going that way too."

Taking heart, I went with them to Odawara. That night at the inn they said, "Tomorrow we'll be passing through the barrier station at Hakone. Have you got a travel permit?"[7]

"I never heard of such a thing."

"Give us two hundred coppers, and we'll get one for you."

I did as they said and was let through the barrier station the next day.

All along I remained on my guard, but by the time we stopped at Hamamatsu for the night, I felt I could trust them since they'd taken such good care of me. Before going to sleep, I took off all my clothes. In the morning when I woke up and looked by my pillow, I saw that everything was gone. During the night, they had stolen my kimono, my pair of swords, and the stomach band containing my money. I was stunned.

I asked the innkeeper if he had seen the two men. He said, "Oh? They said they were going on ahead to be in time for the festival at Tsushima Shrine in Owari and that you were to catch up." Completely overcome, I burst into tears.

The kind innkeeper tried to console me. "You know what they were? 'Flies on sesame seeds'—thieves that prey on travelers.[8] And here I'd thought they were your companions from Edo. What a shame! Where will you go now?"

"I'm not sure—I was thinking of going somewhere near Kyoto."

"Yes, but what can you do, with only an underrobe to your name?"

The innkeeper was at a loss, too, but then he disappeared for a minute and returned with a big ladle. "Well," he said, "you're not the only one from Edo who's been robbed on this road. Here, take this, and go to the neighborhood of Hamamatsu Castle and the countryside beyond and see if you can't beg for a coin or two."

I got up my courage and spent the whole day begging. By evening I had received about a peck of rice and wheat and 120 or 130 copper pennies. The innkeeper was a good-hearted man and put me up for the night. The following day he said, "It might not be a bad idea if you first went to Ise Shrine and prayed for your well-being."[9]

I gave him half of the grain and fifty coppers as a token of my gratitude and headed for Ise. During the day, I begged for alms, and after dark I sought shelter in pine groves, on river banks, and in roadside shrines. Swarms of mosquitoes prevented me from sleeping, and believe me, that was no fun.

At Aioinosaka in Ise I became friends with another young beggar. He gave me some advice. "Go to a priest named Ryūdayū and tell him that you've taken time off from the greengrocer Ōsakaya in Shinagawa to pay your respects at Ise.[10] Explain your situation to him and ask him to put you up for a few days. He'll check his records and let you stay."

I went straight to Ryūdayū's residence and delivered a little speech to an attendant at the inner entrance. A man wearing a *hakama* came out. He had a ledger with him, and after looking through it several times, he motioned me to step inside. I entered with a beating heart and sat down as told in a small waiting room.

Before long the man in the *hakama* came back and

*Pilgrims at Ise Shrine.* From *Ise sangū meisho zue.*

まつわうんぱい
末社順拝

前に斎ひたてまつれる<br>
度會郡にそ郷り<br>
産を捨社末社を<br>
妻に此野せ〜<br>
抽かれたる杉籬<br>
月籟を彩る〜の影と<br>
ていく宮中よ<br>
其遙拝所と<br>
まる〜

told me to take a bath—it had been some time since I had last bathed. After my bath the same man brought out an assortment of delicious-looking food. He said, "I'm afraid it's rather simple—" I hadn't eaten for several days, so I stuffed myself until I was ready to burst.

By and by the priest Ryūdayū himself appeared. He was dressed in ceremonial robes. "How admirable of you to come all the way from Edo to make this pilgrimage," he said. "I will present you with an amulet tomorrow." I kept nodding, "Oh yes, yes indeed." He brought out a set of quilts and a mosquito net and bid me good night. I slept in great comfort. The next morning I ate another delicious meal and was given the amulet.

It then occurred to me that I might as well try to borrow some money in case an emergency arose. I spoke to the attendant, and in a few minutes the man in the *hakama* came out. "What can I do for you?" he asked. I told him how I'd been robbed of everything and said, "I wonder if I could have a loan of about two *ryō* for the road?" He said he would talk to Ryūdayū and withdrew.

He returned in a while, and handing me a string of a thousand coppers,* he said, "As you may have noticed, there are many pilgrims staying here with Ryūdayū, and he has little money to spare. This isn't very much, but please take it."

I took the money and made a hasty exit. I visited shrines along the road and filled my belly with all sorts

*The equivalent of about one-fourth *ryō*.

of good food. Very soon I was no better off than I'd been before, or as they say, "the same old Mokuami."[11] The beggar who had told me about Ryūdayū was the son of a papermaker named Murata and came from Kuromon-chō in the Kanda section of Edo.

Heading back to Edo, I begged along the road and finally arrived empty-handed at Fuchū in the province of Suruga. Just think—I wore only an underrobe with a rope for a sash and didn't even have a pair of straw sandals. A fine figure of a beggar I must have been! At the post station in Fuchū there was a small shrine dedicated to Kannon or some other deity. I crawled under the open porch and slept there every night.

One night I slept by a big pile of rocks just inside the entrance to a riding ground near Fuchū Castle. The riding ground bordered on a bamboo grove, and beyond that stood a temple with the shogun's crest on its main gate. Early in the morning I was awakened by fourteen or fifteen samurai who had come to practice riding. They galloped around with an air of fierce determination, but I could tell right away that none of them was any good. As I got up, a couple of the stable boys spotted me and began shouting. "Look, a beggar boy. The nerve of him, sleeping here. What made you think you could come inside?"

I mumbled some excuses and stayed where I was squatting on my heels, but the men were so hopelessly clumsy that I couldn't help laughing out loud. The stable boys were indignant. They set on me with their fists and after knocking me down, dragged me out of the riding ground.

I protested at the top of my voice. "What's so wrong with telling people they're no good when they're really no good?"

A samurai who was about forty came over. "Hey you, beggar boy," he said. "How does a kid like you criticize samurai for the way they ride? Where are you from anyway? Come on, speak up."

"I am from Edo, and I'll have you know, I wasn't always a beggar."

"Do you like horses?"

"Yes—"

"Let's see you ride then."

Clad only in my underrobe, I showed them a thing or two about riding. Everyone was impressed and said to one another, "This wretch must be the son of a samurai." The samurai who had spoken to me earlier said, "Come home with me, and I'll give you a meal."

So after the practice ended, I followed him to his home. It was on a side street near the residence of the Fuchū town magistrate. We entered through a simple gate and went round to the kitchen door. He told me to wait and soon came out with a tray piled high with rice and soup. It was delicious.

The samurai had his own meal in a room further inside. He came to the kitchen afterward and asked my name and who my parents were. When I put him off with some lies, he said, "I really feel sorry for you. Stay with us." He gave me a kimono and had his wife arrange my hair and fill a bucket with hot water for me to wash up with. The two just couldn't do enough for me.

In a while the samurai went off somewhere very

properly dressed in a *kataginu*\* and *hakama*. He came back late in the evening. Now that I think it over, I realize that he was probably a senior policeman[12] in the service of the town magistrate.

That night he called me into the living room and questioned me once more about my background.

I lied again. "My family? They're tradesmen."

"In that case, why not live here? I'll see to it that you get a pair of swords and a *hakama* right away."

I stayed for six or seven days, and the entire time the samurai and his wife looked after me as though I were their own child.

I had different plans, however. What good was it, making do in a house like this when I could just as well go to Kyoto and become a retainer in some nobleman's house? One evening I changed into my old underrobe, and after folding my kimono and obi neatly by the quilts, I slipped out of the house. I spent the night in a roadside shrine on the other side of the Abe River, got up before sunrise, and ran as fast as I could toward Kyoto.

With no money and no food I was in an awful fix for three days. I begged a coin here and there and slept two nights in a Jizō[13] shrine in Utsunomiya.† It was around eight on the second night that I was awakened by a crash somewhere in the vicinity of the shrine veranda. Thinking that another man might be out there, I cleared my throat. A voice called back, "Who's there?"

"A pilgrim on the road to Ise."

\*A sleeveless jacket with stiff, extended shoulders that was worn with a *hakama* for official duty.
†Katsu means Utsunoya Pass near Mariko.

"Good. I was planning to go on to the next post station to gamble. Carry my money for me, and I'll give you something to donate to Ise."

I got up and followed the man to a shed somewhere near the entrance to the post station of Mariko. Inside, thirty or so men were seated in a circle. One of them— he seemed to be the boss—looked at me and demanded, "What's this dirty beggar doing in here?"

The man who had brought me said, "The boy said he was on his way to Ise, so I decided to bring him along."

"All right then. Here, have something to eat and wait around. I'll give you an offering for Ise later on."

The boss treated me to food and sake. After they had gambled for a while, the man I had come with handed me three hundred copper pennies wrapped in a piece of paper. The other gamblers also gave me money—fifty, one hundred, twenty-four, twelve— altogether about nine hundred pennies. "Now go back quickly to the Jizō shrine and sleep for the night," they said. I thanked them, and just as I was about to leave the shed, one of the men called me over and gave me three big rice balls. Overjoyed, I ran all the way back to the shrine, made an offering to the Jizō, and went to sleep.

I wandered for several days begging, and at Yokkaichi bumped into Murata, the beggar who had told me about Ryūdayū. I thanked him for his kind advice and gave him one hundred copper pennies. He seemed very pleased and said, "I haven't had a decent meal for days. Let's get something to eat." We bought food and shared it stretched out on the floor of a pine grove. We talked of all that had happened since we'd last seen each other and spent the night side by side on a bed of pine needles. You've got to admit, the friendship between beggars is something special.

My friend and I made another trip to Ise. He said that he wanted to go on to Konpira Shrine[14] in Shikoku, so we parted at the town of Yamada. I drifted around in Ise for some ten days and headed back for Yokkaichi. One night I slept in a pine grove at Shiroko and came down with a high fever and a splitting headache. I spent the next day in a delirium. It was a couple of days before I finally came to. I managed to make my way to the main road and get several coins from passersby, but I collapsed once again and barely survived on water for the next seven days.

Not too far from the pine grove was a secluded temple. The priest discovered me and brought a bowl of wheat gruel each day. I slowly regained my strength. The priest also gave me two straw pallets, one to use as a mattress and the other as a cover.

Twenty-two or twenty-three days must have gone by. To my great joy I found that I was strong enough to stand up. I made a pair of crutches from a bamboo switch and hobbled around. Within two or three days I was able to go to the temple and thank the priest. He gave me an old sedge hat and a pair of straw sandals and told me to take good care of myself. Then, as I was going out the front gate, he called me back and pressed a string of one hundred copper pennies into my hand.

I limped along, covering at most two miles a day.

Pilgrims on the road to Ise were never given food that was cooked, so I had to get by crunching on grains of raw rice. What with my stomach still in poor condition, I was soon ill again. I crept into a big hole under a bridge—I can't remember where—and slept for five or six days.

One evening two young beggars approached me. "That hole you're sleeping in—someone from Kanda was using it until last month, and now that he's gone, it's ours. Just because we were away for a couple of days, it doesn't mean you can have it."

I explained to them I was sick.

"All three of us can sleep in it then," they said.

We shared the hole for six or seven days. I was short on food, though, and asked the two beggars what I should do. They said, "You won't get anything cooked around here—it's against the regulations of Ise Shrine. Why don't you go to a village farther off?"

I followed their advice and hobbled on my crutches for over a mile. On the outskirts of a village a man carrying a long stick stood guard. "You're not allowed in here!" he shouted. "Can't you see the sign over there? Get out, you scum!" He started to beat me with the stick, and still weak from hunger and sickness, I fainted on the spot. When I recovered consciousness, I found that the guard had kicked me out of the village precincts.

It was all I could do to drag myself back to the hole under the bridge. My two beggar friends took one look at me and wanted to know what had happened. I told them about the village guard.

"Do you have any rice?" they asked.

I brought out the three or four cups of rice and wheat I had saved up.

"All right, we'll cook some gruel for you."

They brought out a chipped sake bottle and filled it with some water and a handful of grains. They next dug a hole in the embankment and after building a small fire with some twigs, set the bottle over the flame to simmer. I swallowed a mouthful or two and gave the rest to the two beggars. Later I found an old sake bottle for my own use and cooked whatever grains I could get. It was a big improvement over my previous diet.

Feeling much stronger, I stumbled on to Fuchū. I didn't have any money, but luckily, it was the season of the Bon festival for the dead.[15] Every night I made the rounds of the town.

One evening in a section called Denma-chō, I saw that a rice dealer had set out a row of small plates of ground grain as alms. I helped myself to one, and noticing another plate with a copper penny, I furtively reached over for that one, too. A man who was pounding rice in the shop saw me. "How dare you take two plates!" he bellowed, and beat me with his fists until I fell unconscious to the ground. I don't know how long I lay there, but I finally came to and limped to a nearby roadside shrine to spend the night. It had been bad enough trying to get around on crutches, but now it hurt even to move. I spent the next day inside the shrine.

Several days passed. I was very hungry. One evening I went to Nichō-machi, but all I could get was some rice and wheat grains. I continued walking until I found myself in front of a brothel that stood on a street corner. Inside, a customer was carrying on merrily. He poked his head out and cried, "Say there, anything the matter—hopping around on crutches at your age? Are you sick?"

"I'm afraid I am, sir."

"Just as I thought. A good thing you didn't die. Wait, I'll get you something to eat."

He had some boiled rice, fish, and other tidbits wrapped in a bamboo sheath and handed me the food with three hundred copper pennies. A sinner who had come face to face with the Buddha himself in Hell couldn't have been happier. I threw myself on the ground and thanked him over and over.

The customer speculated about me with the prostitutes. "From the way he talks, I'd say he comes from Edo. And I'll bet he wasn't always a beggar. From a samurai family, I would guess."

Then, to add to my happiness, he gave me a white cotton kimono decorated at the sleeves with red crepe and a loin cloth made of dark blue crepe. He said, "Now go to a cheap inn and get a good night's rest on the tatami." I thanked him again and went straight to an inn on a side street in Denma-chō.

I begged in the streets of Fuchū during the day and at night returned to the inn. Expenses for food and lodging kept mounting, however, and I soon had to pawn the kimono for six hundred copper pennies. I paid the bill at the inn and clutching the remaining change, left in a hurry for Kyoto.

One day I was lying down by the side of a teahouse on the outskirts of Ishibe when a group of porters carrying chests for the daimyo of Akizuki stopped for a break. Two of the porters came to the teahouse and sat down for some sake. One of them said to me, "I can tell you've been sick. Where are you going, by the way?"

"Someplace near Kyoto."

"Anywhere in particular?"

"Not really—"

"Forget it then. You don't want to go there. Better go back to Edo. I'll take you, but first you'll have to get your hair done up in proper samurai style."

The porter took me to a hairdresser close by. After my head had been shaved and my hair combed into a topknot, he looked me over. "It won't do to have you in those rags," he said, and gave me a clean cotton kimono and a small cotton hand towel. "And we certainly won't get very far with you limping on crutches like that. We'll have to put you on a palanquin."

He hired a palanquin and looked after me every day. I had been told that I'd be taken all the way to my home in Edo, but the night we arrived in Fuchū, the porters got into a big brawl about gambling, and the porter who'd been so kind to me decided to return to Kyushu. He took back the kimono, gave me an old cotton underrobe instead, and departed immediately. The other porter, his friend, felt sorry for me and said, "Consider yourself lucky to have come this far. From tomorrow you'll have to make it on your own." He gave me fifty copper pennies.

I had little choice but to beg again. I wandered listlessly for several days. One night—I've forgotten where—I lay down near a cliff and somehow fell off the edge in my sleep. I must have passed out, too. When I regained consciousness the next morning, I realized that I had hit my testicles against a sharp rock. It was too painful to walk.

I got better little by little and by the third day was able to walk about gingerly. By the time I reached Hakone, however, my testicles had become swollen and were beginning to ooze pus. Gritting my teeth, I pushed on and arrived at Mount Futago late the next day. I fell asleep exhausted.

Toward dawn a mail courier came by.[16] "Did you spend the night here?" he asked.

"Yes—"

"You've got guts then. You could've been eaten by wolves.* From now on you'd better not sleep in the mountains." He tossed me a string of pennies and took off.

I crossed Sanmaibashi Bridge and settled down to nap by the side of a teahouse. Five or six coolies came up to me. "Hey kid. Why are you lying down here?" one of them asked.

"I'm lying down because I'm too hungry to do anything else," I said.

The coolies brought me a lot of food, and as I was eating, one who looked about forty said, "Come to my house and work as a servant. I'll see to it that you get plenty to eat."

I accepted his offer and went home with him. The coolie's name was Kiheiji, and his house was on a side street near Odawara Castle, in a section called Ryōshi-

---

*Ōkami* or wolves, actually wild dogs, were found throughout Honshū into the early Meiji period.

chō. As soon as we were inside the house, he called out, "See here, I've brought a boy home to work for us. Be good to him." His wife and daughter came out and made a big fuss over me. They insisted that I eat and gave me rice that had been stretched out with bean curd dregs together with a huge platter of broiled fish.

A day passed, and Kiheiji said, "Starting tomorrow you can go to sea and help row a boat."

I nodded, for I'd been on boat rides in Edo any number of times.

"By the way, what's your name?"

"Kame."

He handed me a small bowl. "This is for you to pack your lunch. And be ready to leave for work every morning at four. But don't take any food for a couple of days, because someone brought up in Edo like you won't feel like eating the first time out at sea."

"Oh, I'll be all right," I assured him. "Back in Edo I used to go out on a boat practically every day."

"Well, it won't be like the sea at Edo—"

I decided to ignore him and bring my lunch anyway.

Kiheiji took me to the home of a man who would be working on the same boat. I was told to report early the next day.

I worked on the boat every day. Pretty soon the other crewmen were saying to one another, "Kame sure walks in a funny way." And no wonder. My testicles were still swollen and oozing pus. I managed to hide my condition to the end, but it wasn't easy, let me tell you.

We usually returned to shore about ten in the morning. We would haul the boat about three or four hundred yards inland and set out the nets to dry. Then each of us would be given a small share of the day's catch to peddle in Odawara. After that I went home to do chores like buying bean curd dregs to cook with the rice or running errands in the neighborhood. Every now and then I was given two or three pennies.

Kiheiji's daughter, who was about thirty, was particularly nice and bought me watermelon and other treats. Her mother was something of a shrew and never gave me a moment's rest. Kiheiji worked as a coolie and was at home only in the evenings. He was truly a good and generous man and often came out to the kitchen to bring me sweets. In fourteen or fifteen days he was treating me just as if I were his son.

One day, after asking various questions about Edo, he said, "Kame, stay with us and become a member of our family." I thought about his proposal. It had been four months since I'd run away from home, and here I was, a samurai, wasting my time at a job that would never lead to anything. I made up my mind to return to Edo and face whatever punishment my father had in store. I buttered up to Kiheiji's daughter and wheedled an old, patched-up kimono from her.

On the second day of the intercalary eighth month,* I got out of bed about two in the morning, stole three hundred pennies from the shelf, packed my bowl with food, and left the house with the announcement that I was off to work.

I reached the outskirts of Edo around two early the following morning. Unfortunately, the sky was dark,

*A month inserted into the lunar-solar calendar, which was made up of months of twenty-nine or thirty days, to adjust to the solar year.

and as I passed the prison at Suzugamori, a pack of dogs surrounded me.[17] When I yelled frantically for help, a couple of prison guards came out and shooed the dogs away.

At Ryōshi-chō in Takanawa I found a boat—the kind used for gathering seaweed—and turned it over me and went to sleep. I must have been very tired. I slept well past sunup, until I was roused by the angry shouts of some men in the neighborhood who had discovered me. I mumbled some excuse and hurried away. Stopping only to buy food, I arrived at Atagoyama* and slept for the rest of the day. After nightfall I pretended to leave the grounds and hid under a clump of trees.

For several days I lay low, hoping that no one I knew would see me. On the fifth day I went as far as Ryōgoku Bridge. The next day I hid in the graveyard at the Ekōin temple and left only to buy something to eat. I used up my money and had to crawl out under the fence every evening to beg. But not many people were willing to give alms at night, and I was hungry most of the time.

A band of beggars had staked out a corner of the graveyard. The leader asked me to come join them, so I went over and gorged myself on their food. Finally, one day I ventured as far as Kamezawa-chō. My courage deserted me at the last minute, and I retreated to a lumberyard on the other side of Futatsume Bridge for the night.

Three days later I rose early and returned home.

*A small hill and the site of a shrine.

Everyone was excited. "Kokichi's come back! Kokichi's come back!" I went to my room and slept for ten days straight. I was told that in my absence the family had offered up all kinds of prayers and incantations and had even sent a cousin, a nun called Keizan, all the way to Kyoto to look for me.

A doctor was sent for. After examining me, he said, "Now, is there something you want to tell me about yourself below the waist?" My testicles were still in bad shape, but I stubbornly denied any trouble. Within three months, however, they had become so infected that I could no longer move about. I had to stay home for the next two years.

My father reported my return to my commissioner, Ishikawa Ukon-no-shōgen. "It is indeed a shameful turn of events," my father said. "I will see to it that Kokichi retires and that someone is adopted to replace him as head of the Katsu family."

Ishikawa disagreed. "If Kokichi hadn't returned by the end of the month, I would have taken measures to end the family line.[18] But he's come back, and all's well that ends well. Leave him be. By the time he's older, he will no doubt have mended his ways and be able to perform some useful service. For now, take good care of him."

All concerned were mightily relieved, I was told.

# Youth

I was sixteen.* My infection had cleared up. It was decided that I should apply for official service. I went to Ishikawa's residence to pay my respects. In the front hall there was a register for those seeking jobs to enter their names. I couldn't even write my own name and to my great embarrassment, had to ask someone else.

After I had presented myself, Ishikawa said, "Tell me about your experience as a beggar. Keep back nothing." I told him everything from the very beginning. "Well," he said, "you might say it was a kind of toughening-up experience, and you came through all right. I'll see to it that you get an appointment soon. Be patient."

Meanwhile, the old granny of the Katsu house hadn't changed a bit. She was worse, if anything. "You really went out of your way to ruin the Katsu family, didn't

*Bunka 14 (1817).

you," she said, and accused me of other offenses as well. I stayed away from home as much as possible.

At my brother's office in Edo there was a man by the name of Kuboshima Karoku. One day he tricked me into going with him to the pleasure quarters in the Yoshiwara. I enjoyed myself immensely and after that went every night. I used up all my money. Just as I was wondering what to do, the annual tax money—about seven thousand *ryō*—arrived from the shogunate land under my brother's jurisdiction in Shinano. My brother ordered me to guard the money until it was delivered to the shogunate treasury. I kept an eye on the funds, but then my friend Karoku suggested, "Without money it isn't much fun in the Yoshiwara, is it? Go ahead and steal one hundred *ryō*." "Not a bad idea," I said, and prying open the strongbox, I removed two hundred *ryō*.

The box rattled rather suspiciously afterward, but Karoku fixed that by putting in some stones wrapped in paper. The two of us went about our business looking very innocent. Several days later my brother Hikoshirō discovered the theft, and when he angrily cross-examined everyone, the damned errand boy blurted out that I had stolen the money. My brother kept after me to return the two hundred *ryō*. I denied any knowledge of the missing money and refused to admit to any wrongdoing.

My brother went to my father to complain. My father said, "Hikoshirō, don't you remember getting into trouble now and then when you were young? What's the point of ruining Kokichi's future over a

*Courtesans of the Yoshiwara*. Watanabe Kazan (1793–1841).

little bit of money? See if you can't do something about
it."

It was plain as day that I had stolen the money. All
the same, everyone looked the other way, and the incident was passed over. As for the two hundred *ryō*, I
spent it all in the Yoshiwara in less than a month and
a half. After that I had to scrounge from the rice agents
at the shogunate warehouse and other moneylenders.[19]

I went to Banba-chō one day to visit my cousin Chūnojō. I spent the entire time talking to his sons, Shintarō and Chūjirō. We were joined for a while by Genbei,
a retainer in the household who had a reputation as a
skilled swordsman.

"Kokichi-sama," Genbei said, "I understand you are
rather wild at times and get into scrapes. But have you
ever been in an honest-to-goodness fight? If I may say
so, that takes real guts."

"Oh, plenty," I answered. "I've been in fights ever
since I was a kid, and I've enjoyed every single one."

"Splendid. Because Hachiman Shrine in Kuramae is
having a festival the day after tomorrow, and there's
sure to be a big fight. Why don't you come with us
and test yourself?"

I promised to go and then went home.

On the day of the festival I went to Banba-chō early
in the evening. Shintarō and Chūjirō were waiting for
me eagerly. "Ah, you've come. Genbei's at the public
bathhouse—we'll leave as soon as he's back." Genbei
returned while we were getting ourselves ready.

On the way to Hachiman Shrine we discussed what
we would do if we ran into any trouble. All those who
crossed our path hardly seemed worth fighting, but

once we entered the shrine precincts, a couple of sharp-looking characters sauntered up to us humming a tune. Without warning, Chūjirō spat in the face of one of the men. Outraged, the man lunged at us with one of his wooden clogs. I punched him right in the jaw. At this the other men came at us swinging their fists, but when we hit back in a blind fury, they took to their heels.

We strolled around the shrine grounds. We then noticed a group of about twenty men, all armed with long, hooked spears.

"What the—" As we were wondering aloud, one of the men pointed to us and cried, "Over there—they're the guys!" Finding ourselves quickly surrounded, we drew our swords and flailed madly. Genbei shouted, "Let's get out of here while we can. If they shut the gates, we're lost."

Four abreast we slashed our way out of the shrine grounds. But waiting outside the gates was a reinforcement of some thirty men with pike poles. We were four against fifty. We fought desperately, with our backs to the door of a noodle shop at the entrance to Namiki Street.

Our opponents seemed to slacken after we'd wounded four or five of their men. We fought even more furiously and struck down about ten of the pike poles. Just then more men arrived carrying a ladder.

"There's no use in fighting anymore," Genbei said. "The three of you escape to the Yoshiwara—I'll fight them off by myself. Hurry!"

We felt we couldn't leave him like that. "No, we'll stay with you. We can all escape together."

"Listen, if anything happened to you it would be

terrible. Get away now while you can." Genbei was insistent.

I handed Genbei my long sword in exchange for his shorter one, and without further ado the four of us plunged into the midst of our opponents. As they backed off, Shintarō, Chūjirō, and I made a dash for it. We reunited at the Kaminarimon gate in Asakusa and headed straight for the Yoshiwara. But we were still worried about Genbei, so we returned to my cousin's in Banba-chō for a bite to eat. To our relief and amazement, there, in the front hall, was Genbei, calmly drinking sake!

Together we went back to Hachiman Shrine. A crowd had gathered in front of the guard station at Hatago-chō. We asked what had happened.

"There was a big fight at Hachiman," a man began to explain. "It all started when some guy hit a porter. Twenty or thirty of his fellow porters and about thirty workers from Kuramae got together and tried to catch the guy and his cronies. They couldn't get anyone, and besides, about eighteen of their own men got hurt. There's the doctor, stitching up their wounds—" We left on the spot, and I headed straight for my home in Kamezawa-chō.

Talk about a close call—I was never so scared in my life.

A sword is a samurai's most prized possession and should be chosen with great care. The blade of my sword, made by one Seki no Kanetoshi, was broken about three and a half inches from the guard after I'd lent it to Genbei. So after that I went about learning how to appraise swords.

In the fall I went with Hikoshirō to his office in Shinano and returned to Edo toward the end of the eleventh month.

I continued to practice my skills in fighting under Genbei's tutelage and became quite adept. In one big fight—it was the seventeenth day of the twelfth month, and I'd gone with my usual companions to the fair at Asakusa—Chūjirō was slashed in the shoulder.[20] The blade went straight through to his underwear, but protected by layers of clothing, he wasn't even scratched. He went to sleep that night unaware of the damage.

The maid discovered the tear the next morning as she was hanging up his clothes on the hearth rack. She promptly reported it to his father, Chūnojō. I received a message to come at once to Banba-chō. Chūnojō sat the three of us down before him. He delivered his opinion on the matter and made us sign a pledge never again to take part in a fight. Chūnojō, I should add, was known for his extremely virtuous character and regarded with awe by all his relatives as "a veritable sage."

It was New Year's. I went to Banba-chō to visit Chūjirō and Shintarō. The two were in the garden practicing their fencing. They asked me to join in, but the moment I tried out with Chūjirō, I received a stunning blow in the torso and fainted. As soon as I recovered, I tried again and again, but to my chagrin I failed to hit him even once. So after talking it over with Chūjirō, I decided to study fencing with his teacher, Master Danno Gennoshin of the Jikishinkage-ryū school. My former teacher was put out and made a lot of noise about it, but I paid no attention.

I was eager to improve quickly and threw myself into practice. The following year I was initiated into two secret techniques. No longer at the mercy of every blow, I started going to a Jikishinkage-ryū practice hall. All the students sought me out saying, "Kokichi this" and "Kokichi that." I also engaged heedlessly in matches with students from rival schools of fencing. This was frowned upon by teachers at the time, when fencing was not as popular as it is now, and since most students refrained, I found that they were usually no match for me.

It was the year I was eighteen.* I went with Shintarō and Chūjirō to request a match with Ikue Masazaemon, a master of the Ittō-ryū school who lived in the Uma-michi section of Asakusa. He consented right off and led us to his practice hall. I was matched against one of his students, and as it was my first try there, I fought with all my might and won handily.

We went through a series of matches, and it came time for Chūjirō to pit himself against Masazaemon. He struck Masazaemon right in the torso and sent him reeling against a wooden door. The door fell out, and Masazaemon landed on his back. As he struggled to get up, Chūjirō dealt him several blows on the belly.

We decided to call it quits. But I was still angry at Masazaemon for the way he'd boasted in the beginning, so on the way out I ripped off his name plaque in the

---

*Bunsei 2 (1819).

front hall and took it with me. Later the same day we went on a spree.

On another occasion I went with my friends Kamio, Fukazu, and Takahama to the home of Yamaguchi Sōma in Bakuro-chō to request a match. Sōma invited us in but began to treat us in a condescending manner. Then, when we asked for a match, he had the gall to say, "Not this evening. Come back some other time." To get even, Takahama slashed the curtain hanging in the doorway and flung it inside.

By now all the students in Shitaya, Asakusa, and Honjo who engaged in matches with rival schools were taking orders from me. I stuck a two foot eight inch sword at my side and swaggered about as though I were a regular swordmaster. One by one, the leading students of masters like Inoue Denbei—he had a great many at the time—Fujikawa Chikayoshi, and Akaishi Fuyu, not to mention Master Danno, became my underlings. We went around challenging everyone to matches, and by good luck we always won. Yes—you could say that I was responsible for the new vigor and popularity of other schools of fencing.

The following summer Tatewaki, the son of Nakamura Itsuki, a Shintō priest who presided at the Amanomiya Daimyōjin Shrine in Kakegawa in Tōtōmi Province, came up to Edo. I put in a good word for him when I heard that he was trying to enroll at the school of Ishikawa Seheiji. It seems that during a visit with Tatewaki and his family, Ishikawa had fought a match with Tatewaki's teacher—somebody named

Hayata—and trounced him soundly. Puffed up with success, he had then apparently sat Hayata on his knee and taught him how to handle a spear. Tatewaki had taken all this in and thoroughly convinced that Ishikawa was a master swordsman, had come all the way to Edo to study with Ishikawa. Everyone knew that as far as fencing teachers went, Ishikawa was the very worst, but what can you expect of a country bumpkin? In any event, Tatewaki worked hard, received a certificate, and went back to Kakegawa.

That same year I went again to Shinano. My brother, who was in poor health at the time, sent me to the village of Sakaki to determine the rice tax for the coming year. I deliberately chose a measuring rod's worth of the poorest paddy in the village as a sample. It yielded a mere 1.25 *shō* of rice. I ordered half of that amount as the tax to be paid on all the paddy fields in the village.[21] The peasants were delighted.

About the same time, a samurai named Sakurai, a kinsman of Nitta Manjirō in Kōzuke Province, tried to wheedle some money out of the peasant officials who worked at the district office. A heated argument broke out, and Sakurai drew his sword and wounded a peasant. A posse was rounded up to capture him, but no one dared to go near Sakurai, who had stationed himself at the office gate and threatened to slice anyone who came near with his two foot six inch sword. Several retainers were dispatched from my brother's office, but they, too, were frightened off and stood about wringing their hands.

My brother said, "Kokichi, go get Sakurai." I ran to the spot, but with only four feet between Sakurai and the gate, I realized that it would be impossible to reach him. I would have to think of something quickly. Just then an outcaste in the village came up to me and said, "Sir, I have a plan."[22] He charged at Sakurai with a six-foot pole. The pole was immediately cut in half, but while Sakurai was still holding his sword aloft, the outcaste grappled with him. The outcaste was slashed from his waist to his crotch. In that same instant I flung a handful of sand into Sakurai's face. Blinded momentarily, he lurched forward. The outcaste grabbed him by the testicles and pulled him to the ground. A couple of other outcastes jumped on Sakurai and bound him with a rope. He was thrown into the office jail and further negotiations were conducted directly with his kinsman Nitta in Kōzuke.

The outcaste who had been wounded came from the village of Sakaki. He was rewarded by the government with a generous stipend of about thirty-two bales of rice a year—more than enough for the support of his family for the rest of his lifetime. A cripple for life, true, but as fearless a man as you'll ever find.

My brother kept me busy, sending me here and there to assess the rice crop. Then one day we received word that our mother had died. We hastily finished what official business there was left and set out for Edo. On the way, at Oiwake in Shinano, my brother noticed that a man with a half-shaved pate had surreptitiously joined our group and hidden himself among the stable boys. He ordered me to seize the intruder.

I took an iron truncheon from the side of the palanquin and went looking for him. As soon as he saw me,
he broke into a run in the direction of Mount Asama.
I chased him, but when I'd finally caught up with him,
he put his hand on his long sword and said, "Honorable
official, please let me escape."

"Let you go? Never!" I edged closer. He drew his
sword about a foot, but I noticed that the tip of the
scabbard had gotten caught in his rain cape. I immediately hurled myself at him, grabbed the handle of his
sword, and turned a somersault. We both tumbled to
the ground, with the man landing on top. At that
moment, Kitōji, a peasant official from the village of
Hiraga, arrived and taking hold of the rascal by the
head, turned him over. I shook myself free and gave
the man a beating with my truncheon. Kitōji and I
tied him up and led him back to the post station at
Oiwake.

By and by officials from the shogunate offices at
Ueda and Komoro came to take custody of the fellow.
We were told that his name was Otokichi and that he
was a gambler with as many as a hundred followers.
He had evidently been locked up for two hundred days
in Komoro prison, but he had escaped one night and
gone to Oiwake. We had caught him just after he'd
forced his way into a brothel and talked them into
giving him one *ryō*.

Otokichi was eventually handed over to the shogunate office in Nakanojō rather than to the local daimyo, who, we were certain, would have beheaded him.
My brother said that I could keep Otokichi's sword.
It was a fine specimen, forged by Ikeda Kijin-maru

Kunishige and measuring two feet eight inches. I used it as my everyday sword.

We resumed our trip. During a rest at Usuitōge Pass, a young samurai in the service of an elder of the Komoro domain behaved very rudely to us. I and a retainer, Shiozawa Enzō, picked him up bodily and slammed him against his master's palanquin.

Another incident took place at Annaka in Kōzuke. For some reason a local swordsman suddenly bared his sword and attacked Tsunezō, one of our men. That time, too, Enzō and I overpowered him and tied him up with a rope. When we handed the fellow to the officials at the Annaka post station, we were told that he'd probably had too much to drink.

We arrived in Edo early in the eleventh month. Once again I roamed about, challenging students of other schools to duels.

A fencing master named Kondō Yanosuke lived in the Warigesui section of Honjo. He had a student, Kobayashi Hayata, who had a reputation as a bully who terrorized everyone in sight. One day Kobayashi slyly suggested to Ono Kenkichi, a known rowdy in the service of the Tsugaru domain, to challenge me to a match. Kenkichi turned up at my house. I had heard that he was considered one of Nakanishi Chūbei's top students, but even so, I found his bragging hard to take. At one point the damn fool thrust his sword at me and said, "Just look at it. There's nobody in the entire domain of Tsugaru who owns a sword like this."

I picked it up and examined it closely. The sword had been made in the province of Sagami and was at least two feet seven and a half inches long. I murmured a few words of praise, only to hear him brag again. I got up and showed him my own—the three foot one inch sword that had been given to me by no less than Master Hirayama Shiryū. Kenkichi flinched at the sight of it, so I took the opportunity to indulge in some boasting myself.

"Let's have a match," I said. The coward at first declined. "All right, but not today," he finally agreed. We settled on a date for a match at Kenkichi's practice hall.

I alerted my fellow swordsmen in Shitaya, and on the appointed day forty or fifty showed up. Kenkichi, however, was nowhere to be seen. I sent a note to his home, and a reply came back saying that he'd come right over to my house. I waited at home, and the big bully Kobayashi himself turned up rigged out in formal clothes. He tried to smooth things over.

"Can't you overlook this—I'll see to it that Kenkichi apologizes."

"You're sure of this?"

"Oh yes, and if by chance Kenkichi bothers you in the future, Katsu-sama, this head on my shoulders is as good as yours."

I let it go at that. After this incident practically all of Honjo came under my control.

A feud broke out among the public bathhouse operators when one of them announced that he was moving his establishment from Shiba Katayamamae to Mukō-machi. A priest at the Zōjōji temple had offered to secure the good offices of the town magistrate Saka-

kibara and received twenty *ryō* from the grateful bathhouse operator. Nothing but a hoax, of course. When
the unsuspecting bathhouse operator applied to the
magistrate's office for permission to move, the officials
would have nothing to do with him, saying that public
bathhouses were the concern of Taruya San'uemon and
that furthermore, he had neglected to observe the proper
procedure. The operator was in great distress.

A friend, Nakano Seijirō, came to see if I could help.
I said, "Fortunately, the daughter of a cousin of mine
has married into the Taruya family. I am on good terms
with her father, Masaami, so I'll see what I can do."
Nakano was overjoyed and several days later came by
the house with the bathhouse operator.

I went to see Masaami and after explaining the situation to him, persuaded him to take care of the matter.
In due course an application was issued by the magistrate's office, a hearing held among all parties concerned, and the operator given permission to move.
Jubilant, he gave thirty *ryō* to Taruya, twenty to
Masaami, and forty to me. Nakano said later that the
stock of the bathhouse was held by the mistress of a
man in the service of Sakai Saemon and that the move
to new premises was expected to increase its value by
eighty *ryō*.[23]

That year I accompanied my brother Hikoshirō to the
village of Suibara in Echigo Province, where he had
been newly assigned as district administrator.[24] I toured
the entire territory under his jurisdiction and had a
very good time. For one thing the peasants in the area
were well-to-do, so I got to see all kinds of rare and

costly objects. For another I was given a lot of money and kimono to take back with me to Edo.

Back in Edo I learned that Kobayashi Hayata had switched from Kondō Yanosuke's school to the Otani school and that he was working hard at fencing.[25] He was also still bullying everybody and lording it over his fellow students. I was of a mind to teach him a lesson, but I had to stay in bed with a bad cold, so I let things be for the time being.

Feeling better one day, I went to the practice hall to attend the midwinter session. Kobayashi came up to me. "Katsu-sama, may I request a match?"

"As you see, I've been sick and haven't even gotten around to having my head shaved properly. But since you ask, I'll oblige."

I won the first round easily and the second also. Kobayashi threw down his sword in disgust and tackled me. I pulled him across my hip and threw him to the floor. He went sprawling on his back. I planted my foot on his belly and pointed my sword at his throat. Kobayashi got up and tore off his guard mask. He was mad with rage. "How dare you put your filthy foot on a samurai!"

"Hah! I'm glad you said that. Didn't you say something about since this being our first match, how you, a rank amateur, would like some instructions? Well, I was only showing you what the winner does after he's beaten a fellow samurai in a match. Any objections?"

"Oh no, none at all. You are quite right."

After that, Kobayashi shadowed me around, looking for a chance to ambush me. Now and again he would catch me off guard on a deserted street and tear my *haori* with his sword, but he never so much as scratched me. He wouldn't give up, though, and I had to remain watchful.

One day toward the end of the year—I'd gone to a relative to borrow money to pay off my debts—a very drunken Kobayashi suddenly came reeling out of a side alley. He thrust his sword right under my nose. It was broad daylight, and a crowd quickly gathered around us. I tucked my hands into my kimono sleeves and said, "Well, well, what are you up to, waving your dull old sword at this time of the day?"

"I just bought this sword, you see, and was wondering if you could tell me what you thought about the blade."

I looked at it. "Should cut right through the bone—"

Kobayashi returned the sword to its sheath and walked away—a scoundrel, if there ever was one.

At eighteen I took a wife and moved to a new house on my brother's property in Kamezawa-chō.[26] For the occasion he gave me someone's promissory note for three hundred *ryō* and the rent from the same man's house. My father gave me a complete set of household furnishings. I was pleased to be free of debt, but what with so many people sponging off me, I was in debt again in no time.

I turned nineteen.* I went to the Otani practice hall for the first fencing session of the new year. Higashima Jinsuke and Hirakawa Sakingo got into a fierce argu-

*Bunsei 3 (1820).

ment and challenged each other to a duel outside. As always I broke up the fight and talked them into making up. I was now ordering the swordsmen in the area as though they were my underlings. I sent them off to the provinces to improve their skills, and since they all claimed to be my students, my name gradually spread far and wide. I demolished every good-for-nothing in my own neighborhood of Honjo. Everybody obeyed me. I feared absolutely no one. But all this took a lot of money—appearances had to be kept up—and I fell further and further into debt.

Challenging students from rival schools was getting to be a regular occupation. Night after night I roamed the streets with my followers in tow. Every so often, just to keep them in their place, I took them to the home of Master Hirayama Shiryū to hear him tell stories of heroes of China and Japan. My foolishness was dragging me deeper into debt. I wouldn't stop, even then, and borrowed money with no prospect of being able to repay.

I was twenty-one and penniless. I had no choice but to sell my everyday sword—the Morimitsu I'd bought for forty-one *ryō* from the dealer Owariya Kumeuemon. At the last moment I couldn't bear to part with it. Even to make an appearance at the commissioner's house, I had only the clothes on my back. To take my mind off my woes, I went to the Yoshiwara.

# I Run Away Again

I decided to run away again. I pawned what possessions
I had, including the sword my father had given me,
borrowed from fellow swordsmen, and managed to
scrape together three and a half *ryō*. The night before
my escape I made another visit to the Yoshiwara. In
the morning I went to the Inoue practice hall at Kurumazaka, borrowed a set of fencing gear, and took off
immediately for the Tōkaidō post road.

I walked and walked until I was ready to drop. I
stayed the night at Fujisawa and got off to an early
start the next day to look up my old friend Kiheiji in
Odawara. He was puzzled at first, for how was he to
know that the samurai standing before him was the
young beggar he'd befriended long ago? He finally
recognized me when I said, "Remember me, Kame,
the boy who worked for you and left without saying
good-bye?"

Kiheiji invited me in, and as we were having food
and sake, I confessed how I'd stolen three hundred

copper pennies. I gave him a little over a half *ryō* and added an extra one-eighth *ryō* so that my cronies from my fishing days could join us for sake. When I told them laughingly that I'd become a professional swordsman, they were flabbergasted. They urged me to stay for the night, but I was anxious to go on to Hakone— any moment someone might come from Edo in hot pursuit.

Kiheiji and several of the men insisted on coming as far as Sanmaibashi Bridge to see me off. I waved them good-bye and headed for the barrier station at Hakone. Of course, I had no travel permit. I walked up to the outer veranda of the office.

"Excuse me, sir. I am a swordsman traveling through the provinces to improve my skills. Would you kindly let me through?"

"Show us your papers," one of the officials said.

"As you can see, I am dressed for the streets of Edo. The idea of going to the western provinces came to me on the spur of the moment, just as I was leaving the practice hall. I'm afraid applying for a travel permit was the furthest thing from my mind. Look, I have on only my rush sandals, with no traveling clothes to speak of. I beg you to let me through."

A man who looked as if he might be the head official said, "It is decreed by the shogun himself that no one without a travel permit may pass. But if what you say is true, and you are indeed traveling to improve your fencing, we will make an exception. Be prepared the next time."

"Most grateful, so very kind of you—" I hurried through the barrier station and sat down to catch my breath. A tradesman who was also traveling overtook me.

"Young sir," he said, "as I was going through the barrier station, I overheard the officials talking about you. They were wondering what kind of samurai you were. They knew you weren't a courier and were quite certain you weren't in the service of a daimyo."

"Well, why shouldn't they be puzzled? I am an honorable daimyo." That took care of him.

Nightfall came early in the mountains, and although the touts at the inns pestered me to spend the night, I was determined to cover the ten miles to Mishima. It was the last day of the fifth month, with no moon overhead to guide me. I took off my sandals, tucked them in my waistband, and picked my way through the dark. It was midnight by the time I arrived in Mishima.

I rapped on the door of an inn. "Let me stay for the night."

"Under orders from the district administrator at Nirayama, we are not allowed to put up anyone traveling alone," someone answered.

I went to the transport office of the post station and woke up one of the men to see if he could arrange for me to stay at the inn.

"We can't do that—against official orders."

"Are you telling me that a retainer in the service of Harima-no-kami of Mito[27] can't stay at an inn on the Tōkaidō? I'll have you know that I am on official business, entrusted with a request for prayers at Amano-miya Shrine in Tōtōmi. But if that's what you say, I suppose I shall have to go back to the residence of the post road magistrate and take it up with him. I'll be leaving my baggage here in any case, so keep an eye on it, would you." I tossed my fencing gear through the door into the front room. At this several officials came out in a fluster and threw themselves on the earthen floor.

"Oh, if we had only known that you were from Harima-no-kami—please forgive us for our rudeness."

I decided to press them further. "I'll be leaving my things here for the time being. Give me a receipt."

This upset them even more, and now several other officials came out groveling. "We'll do anything you say. But first, won't you please rest at the inn for a while?"

"Show the way."

They conducted me to the inn annex, all the while apologizing for their oversight, and brought out some food. "Please understand," they pleaded in one voice. "If you don't forgive us, we'll lose our jobs." No longer put out, I said I would forgive them. The officials plied me with more food, but when I asked again for a receipt, they seemed loath to hand it over. So for a second time I pretended to be angry, and this time they tried to placate me with money—one and a half *ryō* to be exact. It was entirely unexpected. I took the money and let it go at that.

By now it was nearing daybreak. Although I hadn't slept a wink, I felt it was time for me to leave Mishima. The officials furnished a palanquin, and I was able to sleep all the way to the next post station. All in all, things had worked out nicely. And why not? Just after leaving Hakone, I'd tied a tag marked "Mito" to my fencing gear.

Of one thing I was certain—I had nothing to fear, for in setting out on my travels around Japan, I had resolved that if need be I would die by the sword.

I arrived at the banks of the Ōi River. The water level was dangerously high, and the coolies were charging ninety-six pennies to carry passengers across. I went to the office for river coolies and called out, "I am on urgent business for the domain of Mito. Take me over at once." A coolie came hurrying out. "Very important business," I repeated. "I am the honorable Harima-no-kami." I gave the coolie the fee for one passenger. My baggage was taken separately, while I myself was carried high over the swirling waves on a litter borne by four coolies. It was most agreeable.[28]

I was now at the post station of Kakegawa in the province of Tōtōmi. I knew that Nakamura Tatewaki lived nearby, and remembering how I'd once done him a favor, I decided to visit him. Walking up to the transport office, I said, "I am on my way to see Nakamura Itsuki, the head priest at Amanomori Shrine.* I must deliver a request for prayers from the Mito domain. A palanquin, if you please." One was provided right away.

I was taken to Mori, a post station on the Akiba post road. As soon as the station officials heard from the bearers that I was an emissary from Mito, they

*Katsu means Amanomiya Shrine.

dispatched a messenger to the Nakamura family. Father and son arrived within minutes. When I poked my head out of the palanquin, Tatewaki's mouth fell open.

"Katsu, what in the world are you doing here?"

"I'll explain everything—wait till we get to your house."

At his house Tatewaki's father thanked me warmly for looking after his son in Edo. I told them what I'd been up to lately. "And then, when I got to Kakegawa, I thought of you and decided to pay a visit."

"Well, you must stay as long as you like," they said, and gave me the use of the sitting room.

The family saw to my every comfort. I made myself at home, engaging in matches at the local practice hall and doing whatever I pleased. Soon I had four or five students lined up. I gave lessons every day. It seemed pointless to stay much longer, however, and I had just about made up my mind to go on further west when an itinerant swordsman from Chōshū called Jōichi Sōma passed through the village. We had a couple of matches, but afterward, while I was copying a list of the places he'd visited, he fell sick and asked if he could rest for several days. I couldn't very well leave him, so I spent the time preparing for my departure.

One evening Itsuki took me aside. "I really think you should go back to Edo," he said.

"I appreciate your worrying about me, but I can never go back. You see, this is the second time I've run away."

"Then at least stay here until the end of the seventh month. You don't want to travel in this heat."

Having accepted his hospitality all this time, I didn't

see how I could refuse. The family treated me even more kindly. I was busier than ever, for besides the students in the neighborhood, young men from the surrounding area were turning up for lessons. I was given kimono and money, and all my daily necessities were free, since my students had me charge them to their accounts. In Sakisaka, some seventeen miles away, I had an old friend, Sakisaka Asatarō, who'd been a student of Inoue Denbei in Kurumazaka. As the district administrator he was set up very comfortably and looked after me generously whenever I went for a visit.

Before I knew it, it was the third day of the seventh month. One morning I was tidying up the sitting room in preparation for a visit from Ishikawa Sehei[ji]—Tatewaki's old teacher—when my nephew Shintarō* suddenly appeared. He said, "I've come to take you back to Edo. The family was afraid if anyone else were sent, you'd hack him to pieces. Come back with me for now—after that it's up to you." Itsuki also strongly urged me to go home. I agreed to return and left the next day with Shintarō.

During a stop at the post station in Mishima, Shintarō fainted and threw everyone into a panic. He finally came to, but we rode in palanquins for the rest of the trip.

Back in Edo neither my father nor brother said a word. I returned to my own house with some relief. The following day I was invited by Hikoshirō to a lavish dinner. In the evening I received a summons from my father. I went right away.

*Katsu's second cousin Shintarō had been adopted by his half brother Otani Hikoshirō. See note 25 of notes to the translation.

"Kokichi," he said. "I hope you realize that you've been behaving very badly, because I am ordering you to stay home for a while. I want you to think long and hard about your life. You'll find that the answers won't come easily, so you might as well take your time straightening things out—a couple of years even. And since people ought to have a measure of learning, it wouldn't hurt if you looked at some books, too."

On returning home, I saw that a cage the size of three tatami mats* had been set up in the middle of the sitting room. I was thrown in.

Inside the cage I jiggled the bars and in less than a month had figured out a way to remove two of them. I also reflected on my past conduct and came to the conclusion that whatever had happened had been my fault. I taught myself to read and write and spent hours poring over military manuals. I was allowed to have visitors and looked forward to their news about the outside world. In this manner I was to pass three years— from the fall of the year I was twenty-one to the winter of the year I was twenty-four. It was an extremely painful period.

My father occasionally sent me written advice. I wrote to him one day that I would like to retire and relinquish the family headship to my son, Rintarō, who was now three years old. This was his answer:

"I think that is a bad idea. It's true you've been guilty of misconduct in the past, but I would like to see you serve in some government post, however briefly, and

*A tatami mat measures roughly three by six feet.

put a stop to the gossip about you. I would also like to see you render some filial piety toward your adoptive family. After that you may do as you wish."

What he said, I realized, was completely fair. I sent a note to Hikoshirō saying that I wished to seek official employment. He wrote back, "If you think you can get together the necessary clothes and equipment on your own, that's your affair. For my part I've already spent more than enough on you. I won't help this time."

I happened to be in bed with a big boil on my face. I sent my brother a message that I had no intention of bothering him in the future and got out of the cage. The next day I went to see the agent who handled the Katsu family house and persuaded him to advance me twenty *ryō*. Within ten days I had assembled all the items I would need for work and was ready to present myself at the commissioner's residence.

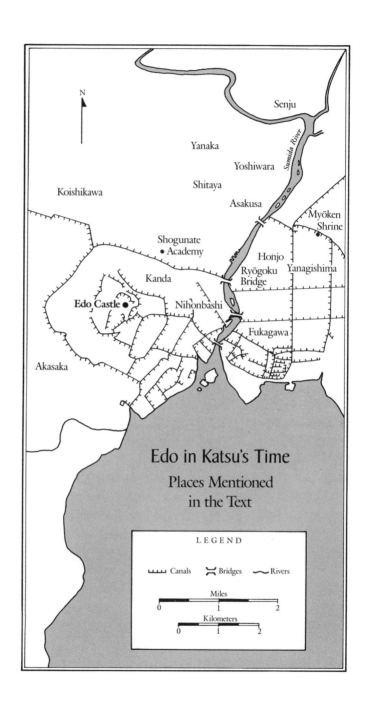

N

Senju

Yanaka

Yoshiwara

Koishikawa

Shitaya

Asakusa

Myōken Shrine

Shogunate
• Academy

Honjo

Ryōgoku
Bridge

Yanagishima

Kanda

Edo Castle •

Nihonbashi

Fukagawa

Akasaka

Samida River

# Edo in Katsu's Time

## Places Mentioned
in the Text

### LEGEND

⊔⊔⊔⊔ Canals    ≍ Bridges    ⌒ Rivers

Miles

0      1      2

Kilometers

0      1      2

# Adult Years

Every morning I put on my *kataginu* and *hakama* and made the rounds of the powers that be.* I went to Commissioner Ōkubo Kōzukenosuke's home in Akasaka Kuichigaisoto and begged him to recommend me for a post. I even submitted a list of the misdeeds I had committed, adding a request that I be considered, now that I had repented. An agent came from his office one day. He said, "Be forewarned that Ōkubo-sama will be sending out investigators to gather information on you." I waited expectantly.

Ōkubo spoke to me one morning. "Your followers simply refuse to tell on you, and though you've confessed everything, we find upon investigating that the mischief you've done is far more serious than you say. Be that as it may, you've repented, and that's good enough for me. I will do my best to get you an appointment. Continue to report diligently."

*Bunsei 8 (1825).

I showed up at his residence with renewed fervor and practiced fencing in my spare time. Often enough my name was entered on the rolls of candidates, but not once was I given a post. And that I found very galling.

I badgered my father and brother into letting me set up a separate residence. I decided to build a house in Warigesui, on the property of Amano Sakyō. I rented the second floor of his house until it was ready.

Sakyō became seriously sick all of a sudden and died. I did what I could for the bereaved family. We moved into our new house. Sakyō's son and heir, Kinjirō, was then only two years old. When the time came to request formal succession to the family headship. Amano Iwazō, a member of the main branch of the family who bore an old grudge against Sakyō, started making things difficult. He tried to have the branch line ended, and with everybody squabbling, it looked as though the matter would never be settled. I was friendly with both branches of the family, so I stepped in and saw to it that Kinjirō was recognized as family head. His family, much pleased, asked me to continue to look after their affairs.

Sakyō's widow now began acting strangely, throwing herself at every man who came her way. It was one scandal after another, and though we'd just settled into our new house, I decided to sell and move out. I applied for permission to the commissioner of Kinjirō's unit. The agent in charge said, "If you leave, there's no telling what might happen to the Amano family. Stay on for a year or so."

I obliged but wasn't happy about it. Fixing other's troubles was all very well, but what about my own? Then one day an old man gave me a piece of advice. "People are wont to repay a good deed with ingratitude. Well, why don't you be different and try returning a good deed for every act of ill will?" I did as he said, and curiously enough, not only did my family situation improve, but even my mean old grandmother began acting more decently. I found, moreover, that people were constantly seeking my help. Whenever a sticky problem or negotiation came up, I dealt with it as though I myself were involved, so that in time even those who had been against me came over to my side, saying, "Yes, indeed. How right you are."

I realized that I owed all this to the old man's counsel. In my happiness I aided fellow swordsmen who'd gotten into trouble or hopelessly into debt, giving them cash or sending them someplace out of harm's way. How many I helped I'll never know, but it paid off nicely years later when I traveled in the provinces. No matter where I went, I was recognized and treated exceedingly well.

Two years had passed since Sakyō's death. His widow was still behaving scandalously. I received permission to move to a house on the property of Deguchi* Tetsugorō, who lived in the same section of town. His oldest son was a friend from way back, and ever since I'd helped him when he had a falling out with his family, his grateful grandmother had been urging me to come live on their land.

*Katsu means Yamaguchi.

I continued to report regularly to the commissioner's residence. I also had to make ends meet, so I tried my hand at dealing in swords and other military accoutrements. In the beginning I lost money—fifty or sixty *ryō* the first month and a half—but I got used to the business little by little, and by attending the second-hand goods market every night, I found I could really bring in profits.

I was anxious to find official employment. But I also had to dash about making money. Then my father died, and I lost heart completely.* His death was entirely unexpected—it seems he'd had a stroke. I was giving fencing lessons at Mazaki Inari Shrine when one of his young retainers came running with the news. I raced to my father's place, but it was too late. I stayed on, helping out, and left the following morning. The next few days were taken up with my father's affairs. My own son was then five. I went back to my business as soon as the mourning period of forty-nine days was completed.

It was in the fall of the same year that I first heard of Yoshida Hyōgo, a Shintō priest of the Marishiten cult in Sarue in Honjo.[29] A number of my friends had taken up Shintō practices under his guidance and were eager to have me join them. I went to visit Hyōgo one day, and we were soon friendly. "Katsu-sama, I understand you have a wide following," he said. "I wonder if you would set up an association for my shrine—I am thinking of calling it the Day of the Boar Association."[30]

*Bunsei 10 (1827).

After agreeing to try, I decided that the members would pay three *mon* plus three *gō* a month. Merchants were invited, as were peasants, not to mention my fellow swordsmen. In a month or so I had lined up about 150 or 160 members. I drew up a list of the membership and showed it to Hyōgo. He was very pleased.

A year and a half later the association had grown to five or six hundred subscribers—all thanks to me. Hyōgo then said to me, "As a propitiation and thanksgiving to the gods, I would like to hold a performance of sacred dances on the Day of the Boar in the tenth month." I called together thirty-eight members who would act as sponsors for the occasion and told them to spread word of the event. I also said that Hyōgo wanted them to come dressed in formal kimono for the edification of the pilgrims and that he himself would be in full ceremonial attire.

On the day of the festivities throngs of pilgrims poured into the shrine grounds. The street in front of the shrine was lined with booths that had been set up by merchants—it wasn't every day you could count on a crowd like this. Members of the association were regaled with food and drink as they arrived. That damned Hyōgo couldn't hold his liquor, though, and was acting up as if he owned a million *koku* of land somewhere off in Nishinokubo. He was also talking rot and nonsense and bossing around my friend Miyagawa Tetsujirō. I lost my temper and bawled him out, and when he answered back with some insulting remarks, I walked off, taking my friends with me.

The following day several members of the association came to apologize. "Listen," I told them, "if it hadn't been for me, this association would've never been formed. And what do I get? Not a word of thanks. The way that idiot Hyōgo goes sounding off, you'd think he'd done it all by himself. You can tell him I'm resigning."

Ōgashira Ihei, Hashimoto Shōhei, and Mogami Ikugorō tried to reason with me. "You have a point there, Katsu-san. But you did go to a lot of trouble to put this association together, and if you leave, everyone else will leave too. Why, Hyōgo is probably regretting it even now and intending to apologize. So forgive him this once, will you?"

"All right, but only on the condition that he write a note saying that he'll never again insult an honorable bannerman of the shogun."

"Oh, we'll make him do anything you say."

They left, and in a while I headed for Hyōgo's place with Miyagawa and Fukatsu Kinjirō. Ōgashira Ihei came part way to meet us. He said, "Hyōgo's put on his ceremonial robes for your visit. He's coming out to the gate to receive you, and then he's going to conduct you to the sitting room and formally apologize for his behavior yesterday. We've made sure of this— so please speak to him."

"Very well."

"And by the way, Katsu-san, the sponsors of the association are holding a banquet in your honor. We'd appreciate it if you didn't mention yesterday's incident."

"As you wish, but you'd better make sure that no one else talks about it either, because if someone does, it'll mean that the sponsors are nothing but a bunch of liars. I'm warning you—I've come today with every intention of cutting down anybody who stands in my way." I said this with particular earnestness and sent Ihei on his way.

Hyōgo and the sponsors were waiting at the front gate. They led me to the sitting room, and after I had taken my place at the head of the room, I put my sword on the sword rack. Everyone sat down. Hyōgo prostrated himself on the floor. "Yesterday, not only did I get drunk but I behaved with extreme rudeness. Please forgive me. I promise to act henceforth with more circumspection."

I said, "You're nothing but a back alley Shintō priest and probably don't know any better. I rebuked you yesterday because you were unspeakably rude to me— an honorable bannerman of the shogun. No sooner does the association show signs of flourishing than you get puffed up with conceit. I advise you to be more careful in the future if you want the association to continue."

With this, the members began fawning on me, pressing me to eat and drink. I don't like sake, so I sat back and watched the others make drunken fools of themselves.

Among those present were Hyōgo's nephew, Ōtake Gentarō. Indignant that I had called his uncle a back alley priest, he had apparently wormed the details of yesterday's incident out of Miyagawa. He burst into the room. "That Kokichi keeps meddling in people's business and just because of his friend Miyagawa, humiliates my uncle in front of everybody. From now on he's going to have to deal with me. Come on,

Kokichi, let's settle it outside." Though still dressed in his formal kimono, Ōtake had bared one of his shoulders and tied a cotton band around his head. When I ignored him, he marched up to me and began making a scene.

"Oh ho," I said. "Ōtake must have taken leave of his senses. Just look at him, wearing a headband like some common roughneck itching for a fight. Samurai should act like samurai, I say, and as one myself, I disapprove of behavior fit for a servant or a sweeper."

"You brazen son of a—" Ōtake picked up a tray and hurled it at me.

I said, "Hyōgo's to blame for this nonsense in violation of our agreement. And seeing how his own nephew attacks me, I'll have to conclude that all this was planned beforehand. All right—I accept your challenge."

"Eat shit!" Ōtake snarled.

Determined to strike first, I reached for my sword. Everyone scurried out of the room, including Ōtake, who bolted for the kitchen. I ran after him but lost my bearings and found myself in a storage room. I was, moreover, unable to get out, for someone had slammed the door and gotten some men to lean against it.

A crowd gathered near the door and began talking at once. They begged me to forgive Ōtake, who, they said, had been scared out of his wits, thrown down both swords, and fled to his home in Iyodonobashi. I said that his behavior was inexcusable. Several others joined in trying to intercede, among them Ōtake's mother. In tears she implored me to forgive her son. I relented and told them to send for Ōtake.

Ōtake came back full of apologies. "I'm afraid I had too much to drink. And considering that we are under the same commissioner, I would be particularly grateful if you didn't report this." I decided to make peace.

Sake was served again. "Have a drink," Ōtake said.

"No thanks. I never touch the stuff."

"Hah, you're not drinking because we haven't really become friends."

Reluctantly I took a sip. Everybody crowded around me and said, "Let's see you drink from a soup bowl." That irked me, so I took a bowlful and emptied it in one gulp. "Just one more, just one more," they all cried. I drank thirteen bowls in a row. By this time the rest of the members were far gone in their cups and behaving like boors. But I remained sober and in perfect control of myself.

Hyōgo ordered a palanquin to take me home. I must have passed out, because I remember going only as far as Hashimoto Shōuemon's house in Hayashi-chō. For three days my throat was so swollen that I couldn't swallow a thing.

The next day some friends came by to report on the latest goings-on at Hyōgo's house. Hashimoto and Fukatsu stayed behind after the others had left. They each brought out a written pledge and said, "We have a request, Katsu-san. From now on please treat us as if we were your kinsmen." After this episode the Honjo area was more than ever under my control.

In my opinion Hyōgo was a thoroughly bad sort. I severed all connections with the association. The other members that I'd persuaded to join left, too, and I heard that the whole thing fell apart.

I went to see Hashimoto Shōuemon on my way home from Myōken Shrine one day. He had a visitor by the name of Tonomura Nanpei. As the three of us chatted about this and that, Tonomura suddenly turned to me and said, "Katsu-san, you must be a believer of the goddess Myōken.[31] Tell me, am I right?"

"Yes—I've been devoted to her for a long time."

"Just as I thought. I could tell from the features on your face."

It turned out that Tonomura not only knew all kinds of strange and marvelous facts but was a practitioner of the Ryōbu Shingon arts.[32] He struck me as an interesting man. Hashimoto asked him about a relative who was very sick. Tonomura said, "I'm sorry to say that your relative has been possessed by a dead person's spirit."[33]

"Have you any idea who it is?"

"The dead person was a male," he said, and went on to describe the man's age, appearance, and manner of death as if he'd seen him with his own eyes. I asked Hashimoto, "What about it?" Hashimoto said the description fit exactly a man he knew. I was terribly impressed and asked Tonomura if he would take me on as a student. He said, "Very well, I shall instruct you as best I can." That same evening I took him home to spend the night.

Tonomura first introduced me to the teachings of the Ryōbu Shingon school and then showed me the correct way to worship Inari, the fox deity.[34] Over the next two months, he taught me how to recite mantras and incantations for the sick, how to communicate with the goddess Marishiten, how to master ascetic discipline, and many other techniques and practices as well. In return I took care of his daily needs—he was somewhat seedy looking—and counting fees and other expenses, in a year and a half I spent close to forty or fifty *ryō* on him.

People came from all over Honjo to study with Tonomura, and he soon had so many students that he had to move to the residence of Ogura Chikara, who lived opposite the Mirokuji temple. He was besieged with requests for prayers and incantations—for the sick and afflicted, for appointment to office, and for every other purpose you could think of. But since I had been the one who had discovered him, he was always happy to oblige me.

Kondō Yanosuke's student, Kobayashi Hayata,* finally became my follower. He came to the house every day and made himself useful in various ways. He had no place of his own, however, so I got a house for him in Iriya in Asakusa, where there were a number for sale. I then told my fellow swordsmen to help him set up a practice hall. It became popular with men around Shitaya, and before long he was able to start a side business as a sword dealer. He was good at it and began lending money to his friends. Kobayashi was also cunning and often cheated his friends unscrupulously. On three occasions he borrowed to the hilt and ran away to Tōtōmi. I will say this for him—he always gave me notice before taking off. On the other hand each time

---

*A lapse of memory on Katsu's part; Kobayashi had already switched to the Otani school.

he came back to Edo, I had to write notes asking his friends to forgive him, and naturally, they were stuck with their losses.

Kobayashi is in Tōtōmi again, having made off with some seventy or eighty *ryō*. He has yet to show his face, but according to Mukōjima no Kane—someone I met in Chōshi—he's more or less shaped up. Kane told me that he met Kobayashi during a pilgrimage to the Hōraiji temple in Akiba. It seems they sat down and talked about me for several hours. He also said that Kobayashi was turned out rather smartly.

One day at Ogura Chikara's house I met a tailor from Kuromon-chō who was in charge of the lots for "shadow lotteries."[35] It happened that my friend Tokuyama Kazue was very keen on lotteries. On the day that lots were to be drawn for the official shrine lottery, he asked Tonomura Nanpei to recite some incantations to invoke the gods. Word got round, and a crowd quickly gathered at Ogura's house, where Tonomura still lived. He was just about to begin when I, unknowingly, dropped by. When it was explained to me that the incantation was to find out the winning numbers in the official lottery, I decided to stay and watch.

Tonomura called in a woman, intoned some prayers, and lit a sacred fire with cedar twigs. He then handed the woman a sacred staff decorated with paper streamers and bade her to commune with the gods. In a while she began to babble. "Today six is the lucky number. Lots sixteen, twenty-six, thirty-six—" All present were delighted. Tonomura started putting things away.

I said to him, "I've never seen anything like this.

I'm quite impressed, but I wonder if it's all that difficult—" The tailor from Kuromon-chō spoke up. "I
realize that it's you, Katsu-sama, and not some ordinary
person who is speaking, but reciting incantations is no
simple matter. There are rules to this, you understand."

"I see what you mean," I answered. "But consider
for a moment. Tonomura here—we've no idea which
horse's rib he's made of or where he's from, and he
manages fine. Now if I, by birth an exalted bannerman
of the shogun, put my heart and soul into it, it stands
to reason that the gods will swiftly heed my prayers.
So when I ask Tonomura something, I'll thank you to
keep quiet."

The tailor was not about to back down. "But Katsu-
sama, I still think it's beyond your powers. In all things
pertaining to the gods, certain rules must be observed."
I strode to the middle of the room and said to the
tailor, "This is no matter for argument. You—get over
here and bow down. And you'd better not raise your
head until I give the word."*

Everyone could see that I meant what I said. They
begged me to forgive the tailor, but when I said I
would, he said, "If you're so sure you can do it, why
don't you try some incantations right now?"

I purified myself with cold water, ordered the woman
to come back, and mumbled some prayers. Sure enough,
the woman began to babble just as she'd done before.
I finished up, made a boast or two, and left. From that

---

*A literal translation of Katsu's words gives the flavor of the original: "If
you raise your head before I give you permission, I'll become your cook
right away." Since Katsu had no intention of becoming the tailor's cook,
the words express a threat.

day on everyone came to me for incantations—I charged less.

Some time later Tokuyama asked Tonomura if he would recite some incantations using his own younger sister as a medium. He was told, "Your sister is possessed by a living person's spirit. It will take at least two or three days to exorcise it, and that will cost five *ryō*." Tokuyama decided to ask me instead. I worked at it for three nights running and finally drove the spirit away.

Tonomura resented my success and broke off our friendship. I joined forces with Tokuyama and on "shadow lotteries" alone made ninety *ryō*. Apart from this we easily made ten or twenty *ryō* any number of times.

I took up religious austerities and penances. I began by going to the Fuji Inari Shrine in Ochiai for a hundred nights. I went next to the Inari Shrine in Ōji for a hundred nights and after that to the Inari Shrine in Handa for another hundred nights. I also carried out the cold water penance. Squatting half-naked in front of the shrine altar, I poured bucket after bucket on myself for five or six hours at a stretch. That lasted 150 days, and much of it during the winter, too. While performing these austerities, I had many interesting experiences, but I won't go into them. Fasting was something else I tried three or four times. I was convinced there was nothing I couldn't do.

The family of my landlord, Yamaguchi Tetsugorō, had served as district administrators, and the space once

*A Swordsmith and His Assistants.* Kuwagata Keisai (1764–1824).

used for their office stood empty. I invited Suishinshi Shūsei, a swordsmith married to a granddaughter of Suishinshi Tenshū, to come and use the space to forge swords. I also invited Kichi, a disciple of Hon'ami Yasaburō, to live in my house and work at his profession of polishing blades. I took a few lessons from him.

It then seemed like a good idea to form a sword association in which members would pay dues and take turns buying a sword. I invited my fellow swordsmen and friends to join, along with Hosokawa Chikara Masayoshi, Minobe Taikei Naotane, Kanda no Michiyoshi, Umeyama Yasohachi, Kobayashi Shinpei, and all the other sword appraisers in business.

One day I went to the shogunate prison in Senju

and tested my sword on the corpses of criminals who had been executed.[36] After that I became a student of Asauemon and learned how to lop off the heads of corpses with a single stroke.

At home, matters were improving, for my son, Rintarō, now seven, was in service at Edo Castle.[37]

My landlord, Yamaguchi Tetsugorō, received only a small stipend and was always short of money. He complained to me that he was being hounded by creditors, so I settled his debts for him. He then complained that none of the nine families living on his property ever paid the house or land rent on time. I threw out the tenants and brought in my friends and acquaintances. The rents now came in regularly, and my landlord went around all smiles saying, "Thank goodness, thank goodness."

He told me one day that he was thinking of petitioning the government for an appointment as district administrator. When I advised him against it, he became very angry and sent me a notice of eviction after consulting Hayama Magosaburō, one of his men. I went to him and explained at length what the position of district administrator involved.

"And look," I said, "you're already past fifty. You would be better off giving up the idea."

"What makes you say that?"

"Well, to serve as district administrator, you'll need at least one thousand *ryō* to start with. Your rental properties in Edo are bound to fall into disrepair, and that will take over two hundred *ryō* to fix. Getting your men properly outfitted will take another one hundred *ryō*, and moving expenses—that's assuming you move to your jurisdiction—will come to over one hundred *ryō*. That's almost two thousand *ryō* already, and let's say that your bailiff is incompetent and you incur liabilities. No matter how frugal you are, it will take at least thirty years to pay off your debts. Your descendants may well suffer, too, because if they don't come up with the money, they'll be banished to some far-off place or may even have their family line abolished. No, it really isn't the kind of job that someone without ability should seek."

The landlord and his family were incensed and demanded that I clear out at once. So I went around to collect the rents that were due and pocketed the money. My next concern was to find a place to live. Unfortunately, my chronic beriberi was making it almost impossible to walk. I had a friend look for me and decided on a house on the property of Okano Mago-ichirō, a samurai in my unit who lived in Irie-chō.

I went to Yamaguchi to give formal notice of my move. I said, "If by any chance you become district administrator, and I doubt you'll last five years even if you do, I advise you to be very careful. Of course, my predictions could turn out to be wrong, but in that case you may count on not seeing me alive."

"And what do you mean by that?"

I told him what I knew about his retainer Hayama Magosaburō and left.

Several years later Yamaguchi was appointed district administrator in Kōshū Province. A riot broke out in his fourth year of office, and just as I'd expected, he failed miserably at the job. He was recalled to Edo and transferred to the Escort Guards.[38] He was, furthermore, three thousand *ryō* in debt and in danger of having his family line abolished. His man Hayama was sentenced to jail for three years.

Feeling sorry for my former landlord, I went to visit him. "And all this because I didn't listen to you," he said with tears in his eyes. "But if possible, I would like to save my family from being disgraced." I pitied him, so after hearing what Hayama had done, I drew up a draft of a letter to be sent to the district office in Kōshū. "Try sending something like this," I told him. "You never know—some generous benefactor might come forward. With at least five hundred *ryō*, I should think."

Yamaguchi looked nonplussed. He nevertheless sent off a letter immediately, and shortly afterward, six hundred *ryō* were delivered from Kōshū. His family was saved from ruin, but his stipend was reduced to forty-three and a half bales, thirteen and a half being handed over directly to a rice agent to whom he owed fifteen hundred *ryō*. Because of all this, his children still visit me every month.

In the end Yamaguchi was demoted to the *kobushin-gumi* and put under house arrest for one hundred days. But Inoue Gorōzaemon, another official involved in the same affair, was stripped of stipend, house, and samurai status. As for Hayama, after serving his sentence, he was banished from Edo.*

*A form of punishment forbidding a person to live within twelve miles of Nihonbashi.

My beriberi was much better since moving to Okano's land in Irie-chō. It must have been a month or so after we had settled in that Rintarō, now nine, returned from service at Edo Castle.* I decided to send him for reading and writing lessons to a retainer in the employ of Tarao Shichirōsaburō, who lived on the other side of Mitsume Bridge.

One morning on his way to lessons Rintarō was bitten in the testicles by a mad dog. Hachigorō, a laborer from Hanamachi, carried him home. Although I was still recuperating at the time, I flew to Hachigorō's house as soon as I received word.

Rintarō was propped up against a pile of quilts. I pulled up his kimono front and saw that his testicles were intact. Fortunately, a doctor called Narita had already been summoned. When I asked him, "Will my son live?" he sounded rather doubtful. I turned to Rintarō and yelled at him. He seemed to get hold of himself, so I called for a palanquin and took him home.

My landlord had sent for a doctor named Shinoda. The doctor began stitching Rintarō's wound, but I noticed that his hands were trembling. I bared my sword, plunged the blade into the tatami near Rintarō's pillow, and drawing myself up, glared down at my son and the doctor. Rintarō didn't even whimper, and the doctor managed to finish stitching the wound.

"How does it look?" I asked.

The doctor said, "I can't guarantee he'll live through the night."

On hearing this, everyone in the house began wail-

*Tenpō 2 (1831).

ing. I yelled at them to pull themselves together and slapped them soundly.

From that night on I visited the local Konpira shrine. Stripped to my loin cloth, I dashed buckets of cold water on my body and prayed for my son. I had Rintarō sleep in my arms and forbade anyone to touch him. I raged and stormed and carried on so that the neighbors were soon shaking their heads saying, "That swordmaster who just moved into Okano's place—he's gone out of his mind ever since his son was bitten by a dog."

Rintarō's wound finally healed, and on the seventieth day he was able to get out of bed. To this day it hasn't bothered him in the least. So mark my words—it's care and attention that heals the patient.

Makino Nagato-no-kami, a relative who had been magistrate of Yamada, was newly appointed magistrate of Nagasaki.[39] That same month the swordsmith Suishinshi Shūsei asked me whether I could do anything for Owariya Kamekichi, a man from the Aki domain who lived in Toranomonsoto in Sakurada-chō. Owariya made his living supervising porters for traveling daimyo and was apparently most anxious to act as agent for Makino. I told Shūsei I would try.

Owariya came to see me presently. He took out fifty *ryō* and said, "This is to buy a gift for Makino-sama— something to his liking." I purchased several items and sent them over to Makino's son, but someone had beaten us to it and been appointed only the day before. I told Owariya about it and offered to return the rest of the money. He wouldn't accept. "No, no, that was a fee—it's yours to keep." There was almost thirty *ryō* left over.

Several years later Kuze was appointed magistrate of Nagasaki. Hoping to do Owariya a good turn, I sent a messenger. He was told Owariya had been dead for some time. So that was that.

My new landlord, Okano Magoichirō, was a rake and a spendthrift. He owed seventeen *ryō* to a teahouse in the Yoshiwara, and unable to pay, was being threatened with a law suit. No one was willing to help him out, though, since this sort of thing happened all the time. He came to see me. I had just moved in and in my ignorance got together some cash for him.

Okano got into debt again, having obtained seventy *ryō* at 5 percent interest a month to buy a prostitute out of her contract.* The trouble was, as security he had handed over the ledger recording the payment of rice taxes by his fiefs. The retainers at home and on his fiefs came to me for advice. I got back the document by putting up as security swords and other goods that had been consigned to me. My landlord, however, made no move to help me get my goods back. I eventually retrieved them one by one, but from then on I was always hard-pressed for cash, and with all my social obligations it was an awful nuisance.

For a while I managed to survive by selling what I had left, but I soon ran out of goods and was forced to sell my own possessions. I hated parting with them— I'd collected them painstakingly over the years—but what else was I to do? I sold off every single item— and at half of the original cost. In the end I was hard put to fork out four pennies. And this entirely because of my landlord.

*The officially permitted rate was 1¼ percent a month.

Okano's wife came to see me secretly one evening. She said, "Magoichirō's loose behavior is causing difficulties for everyone in the family. Katsu-san, could you talk to his commissioner and get him to order Magoichirō into retirement?" I went to talk to the commissioner's agent. "We will first need a written statement about Okano's conduct from his wife," he said. I got one from her and presented it to Nagasaka San'uemon, who then discussed the matter with Nagai Gouemon, the commissioner of Okano's unit. Soon after, Okano received orders to retire. There was nothing he could do about it, really.

Okano's heir, also called Magoichirō, was fourteen at the time. I did everything for him, even taking him to Edo Castle for his formal installation as head of the family. His father by then had taken the name Gōsetsu and become a lay priest.*

The Okano family affairs were still in a mess, however. I took charge, telling the retainers how to go about settling accounts, and succeeded in putting the family finances into shape. Then Gōsetsu began acting up again. He hired a man called Iwase Ken'uemon and by devious means obtained for him twenty *ryō* in cash and a stipend of twenty-two and a half bales of rice. His family once more came to me for help. I brought the matter to the attention of Commissioner Nagai Gouemon, and Ken'uemon was duly fired and replaced.

Young Magoichirō's mother died, and Gōsetsu took the opportunity to cook up some more schemes. I had

---

*A common practice among retired samurai during the Tokugawa period; Katsu himself became one upon retirement. It involved no religious training or discipline.

to settle these, too, and later when he bought a prostitute out of her contract and moved her in, I had to find a separate residence in Yanagishima.

A year went by. Gōsetsu became seriously ill, and as usual I took care of him. He called me to his bedside one day. "I don't think I'm going to pull through," he said. "Would you please look after my son? At least don't abandon him until you've found him a wife and made sure he has a government post." When I gave him my word, he looked very happy. He died the next day.

Again I had to take over and set things in order. But finding a wife for young Magoichirō was proving to be difficult—the mere mention of the name Okano would put off most parents. I finally had to settle for the daughter of Itō Gonnosuke in Ichibei-chō in Azabu.

Magoichirō's mother had said all along that anyone who married her son wouldn't need to bring a dowry. I bargained with Gonnosuke anyway and got him to agree to one hundred *ryō* in cash and a set of household furnishings suitable to a family of Okano's rank and station. When word of this got around, everyone— not least the peasants on his fiefs—was astounded. "Here we've been trying for two or three years to find a bride for the young master," they said. "But all we had to do was to say 'Okano', and people would break off negotiations. Now thanks to you, Katsu-sama, every one of us, not to mention the young master himself, can breathe a sigh of relief. And a dowry, too! We are most grateful."

The Okano family stipend was fifteen hundred *koku*, but for some reason Magoichirō owned not one piece of weaponry. Even to report to his commissioner, he had to borrow a pair of swords each time. Small wonder that no parent wanted to give him a daughter. His house was in a shambles, too. So I summoned the peasants on his fiefs in Musashi and Sagami and over five or six days persuaded them to put up four hundred *ryō*. I had the house repaired and bought personal effects for the numerous household dependents. I also had a house built on the property for his uncle Sennosuke, a lay priest, and procured a concubine for him. The members of the family talked as though I were a god. On top of all this I had the living expenses provided by his fiefs raised from two hundred *ryō* to three hundred, saw to it that his men were assured of a year's stipend so they could take various lessons, and even obtained a horse for his use. It was, I knew, a bit extravagant for a family with a stipend of fifteen hundred *koku* and an outstanding debt of five thousand *ryō*. But since when have fools been known to deny themselves?

Meanwhile I was getting poorer and poorer. With nowhere to turn, I decided to throw myself on the mercy of the goddess Myōken and beg her to save me from my poverty. I undertook a Hundred Days Pilgrimage, performing cold water ablutions three times a day, eating sparingly, and praying with all my heart. Eighty or ninety days went by.

While this was happening, it seems that my friends in Shitaya had gotten together and wondered why I hadn't shown up in the neighborhood for such a long time. When they heard from my man Kobayashi that I was down on my luck, they discussed what they could do to repay me for past favors. They hit on the idea of forming a savings association and inviting me to be a non-paying member, but they thought I would refuse if it were put to me that way and decided instead to ask me to head the association. In any event, Suzuki Shinjirō, a student of Inoue Denbei, came to the house one day.

"Katsu-san, my friends and I are forming a savings association to go on pleasure trips. Most of the work has been done, and we'd be honored if you would serve as the head."

"That's very kind of you, but I will have to decline. You see, I can barely make ends meet, let alone join your group."

"It will fall apart if you don't join—"

"Yes, but I can't even put up the initial payment."

"That's all right with us."

I agreed to join and sent him on his way.

Suzuki returned in two or three days. He set down a big ledger, and placing five *ryō* on the cover, he said, "This is for you. And from now on whenever any business comes up, a member of the association will come by."

Once again Myōken-sama had answered my prayers. I went back immediately to my sword business. At the end of the month I made eleven *ryō* selling a Sukekane of Bizen sword to Matsudaira Hōki-no-kami for Matabei, a clerk at the shogunate warehouse. I got an extra five *ryō* from Matabei as a tip. Every night I went to the secondhand goods markets in Kanda and Honjo, and being a pretty sharp bargainer, I soon set aside a tidy sum.

*A Secondhand-Book Stall.* Kuwagata Keisai (1764–1824).

Many of the friends I'd helped in times of trouble came to me when they had swords to sell. But since they were not knowledgeable about swords, I never had a loss. At the markets I made a practice of spending half of the profits to treat my fellow dealers to buckwheat noodles or occasionally, sake. They addressed me as "Lord and Master" and secretly alerted me beforehand if they heard of a customer coming with a piece of goods.[40]

At the auction market, if I guessed wrong and put in a written bid of fifteen silver *monme* for something worth only three *monme*, the auctioneer would take out my slip of paper from under the straw hat and say, "For Katsu-sama, it's three and a half *monme*," and let me off with a loss of only half a *monme*. To make up

for this, though, even if there were as many as fifty
people, I treated everyone to buckwheat noodles after
the markets closed down. The tradesmen—always ready
to bicker over a single penny—so appreciated my generosity that they ordered special cushions for me to use
at the markets.

My friends were envious. "How is it that the tradesmen fall all over themselves for you?" they asked. When
I told them what I did, they said, "That's no way to
make money." But make money I did—and plenty of
it. My stipend was forty bales and I had a debt of over
350 gold *ryō*. Each time I made a profit, I paid back a
small amount—no greater than the cost of a visit to a
brothel—and within two and a half years, my debts
had dwindled to thirty or forty *ryō*. It was simply amaz-
ing.

I always put giving to others first, helping neighbors
as a matter of course and those in need according to
who they were. Perhaps, because of this, even in the
leanest years of the Tenpō famine, I had one-sixteenth
of a *ryō* of spending money each day.

I also helped tide my friends over through hard
times. This meant I had to work hard, so I attended
the secondhand goods markets diligently and thought
of it as a regular job. I took a commission of 4 percent
on sales, and in three months cleared three and a half
*ryō*. I ordered a sword for myself.

Whenever swordsmen got together I was invariably
seated at the place of honor ahead of even the teachers.
At the one-year memorial match for Master Fujikawa
Chikayoshi, attended by over 580 people, I judged the

contestants of the competing "Minamoto" and "Taira" teams.* I also officiated at the memorial match for Master Akaishi Fuyu—this was at Master Danno's hall—and at the memorial match for Master Inoue Denbei and the formal opening of the Otani practice hall. Whether it concerned a dispute between rival schools, disagreements between fellow students, or initiations into secret techniques, I was the one who was usually called in. For that matter Master Danno made a point of consulting me about initiations at his school. And not one person ever contested my decisions. Stranger still, all the men in Shitaya and Honjo copied me—my taste in swords, my clothes, even my hairstyle!

Back then rules of etiquette were observed with utmost strictness in the practice halls. It was unheard of, for instance, for a master and student to sit down together in the same room. If a master from another school sent word that he was coming, a top student always went to his home to carry his sword and teachers were expected to greet the visitor in the front entrance. Nowadays anything goes. No one pays attention to the rules, and no one seems to mind. Things will change, I suppose. It used to be that only two teams were allowed to compete at one time at fencing matches. Even that rule is often disregarded.

A certain Chichibuya Sankurō lived in Tōrimachi. A purveyor of cloth and sundries to the shogunate, he had lately fallen on hard times. Other merchants had

*Teams are traditionally named after the two leading rival families of the twelfth century and distinguished by their headbands—white for the Minamoto and red for the Taira.

become established as purveyors to the shogunate, and he had little hope of getting any orders. I heard this from my friend Takata Tōgorō, who went on to say that the youngest daughter of the shogun was about to move to Aki Province on the occasion of her betrothal and that Chichibuya was most anxious to be named official purchasing agent.

I persuaded Seyama-san, a lady-in-waiting at the main keep of the castle, to speak to Kurenai-san, the woman who had been put in charge of the trip. Now Chichibuya had confided to me that if he were appointed, he would present thirty *ryō* to Kurenai-san and an equally suitable sum to Seyama-san. Apparently, the moment Seyama-san mentioned this to Kurenai-san, the greedy woman had consented eagerly. She issued an appointment to Chichibuya and, for a start, placed an order in the amount of seventy *ryō* of goods. She also demanded the money.

Chichibuya went back on his word, saying how difficult things were and so on, and refused to show his face. I ordered him to come to my house and said that I would have nothing to do with him in the future. Chichibuya, on his part, had already received an official procurement order and was confident that his appointment would not be revoked. Within a day or two it was revoked, the order was canceled, and Chichibuya was left with a pile of unwanted goods. He came running over with his wife. He gave one apology after another, but I was so put out that I left matters as they were. In the end Chichibuya lost close to forty *ryō*. What's more, his store was razed in a big fire, and from all accounts he now lives in some obscure back alley.

There are plenty like him out in the world. Watch out, or they'll trick you the first chance they get.

My second-oldest brother, Matsusaka Saburōemon, received an appointment as district administrator. We'd had nothing to do with each other for ten years, ever since the big row at Hikoshirō's house over a loan of eight *ryō* he had refused to repay me. One day, quite unexpectedly, he sent me a letter—maybe he'd had a change of heart. "It's a shame we haven't seen each other for such a long time," he wrote. "Come and visit us if you are in the neighborhood." Enclosed with the letter was half a *ryō*. Wondering what to do, I went to Kamezawa-chō to talk it over with Hikoshirō's wife. "Since he's asked, I think you should go," she said.

I left immediately for Saburōemon's house in Hayashi-chō. The entire family came out to greet me and treated me to a delicious dinner. There was a great deal to talk about, and by the time I was ready to leave, my brother and I had pretty much made up. A day or so later Saburōemon's wife sent my wife a note saying how much they had enjoyed my visit.

I saw Saburōemon frequently after that, and when he learned that he would serve as district administrator in Suibara in Echigo Province—the very same job that Hikoshirō had held—I told him what I remembered of the customs of the area, the character of the residents, and the general duties involved.

On the seventh day of the first month, when government offices traditionally opened, Saburōemon's oldest son, Chūzō, was slashed by a ruffian who had sneaked into the house during the night. A messenger arrived with the news, and though I ran all the way to Hayashi-chō, Chūzō was already dead. I had an inkling who the murderer might be, so the next day I went around Koishikawa, but the suspect had apparently cleared out.

Hikoshirō and other relatives asked me to stay at the house in Hayashi-chō for the time being. I slept there every night and returned home in the morning to attend to my business. The investigative officer came on the twenty-fifth, and on the twenty-ninth Chūzō's wife, Saburōemon's wife, and Chūzō's oldest son, Juntarō, were summoned to the shogunate court that handled the affairs of retainers. Kurobe Tokusaburō, Saburōemon's third son, and I accompanied them. We went there regularly about twice a month for the rest of the year.

Once, while waiting in one of the rooms at the court, I got into a big argument with Kamiue Yatarō, a senior policeman in the service of Ōkusa Noto-no-kami. It took three men—the custodian of the court, Kamio Tōemon, his inspector-aide, Ishizaka Seizaburō, and a policeman, Yuba Sōjūrō—to convince me to let him off without reporting it to his lord. The altercation lasted about two hours and sent everyone in the room into such a dither that it was all I could do not to laugh in their faces. Samurai, indeed!

This was the year that Saburōemon made his first trip to Echigo. He asked me to look after his affairs in his absence. I got rid of my debts, took pleasure trips, frittered money away on one foolish thing after another, but I knew enough not to fall into debt again. When Saburōemon returned to Edo, I gave him a full written account. He seemed satisfied.

The same year, I adopted the daughter of my cousin Takeuchi Heiuemon and gave her in marriage to Roku-gō Chūgorō, a student of mine with a stipend of three hundred bales.* About this time Takeuchi's son Sanpei was notified that he had received an appointment. San-pei said he would have to decline, since he would not be able to meet the expenses of the office. I scraped up some money for him and saw to it that he reported the next day to Edo Castle. He was told that he had been made a member of the Great Guard. His father was overcome with joy. "Katsu," he said, "I won't forget this favor as long as I live." Years later, though, he didn't think twice about cheating me.

Toward the end of the year Saburōemon was slated to go again to Echigo. He was worried about his son Masanosuke, however, so I suggested that he take his son with him. He agreed. Before their departure I had a talk in private with Masanosuke about the office in Suibara—what to expect and how to behave, especially since samurai attached to district offices were able to make money during their tour of duty. He listened enthusiastically and promised to thank me properly when he came back.

After Masanosuke and his father had left for Echigo, I remembered that I had forgotten to tell Masanosuke how to go about measuring the rice crop for taxes. I sent off a letter. It somehow got misplaced and fell

*The adoption was an expedient to circumvent the shogunate prohibition against marriages between families of unequal status.

into his father's hands. Saburōemon returned to Edo and showed it to Hikoshirō in great indignation. Hiko-shirō was furious and ordered me to come at once to Kamezawa-chō.

"What ever made you fill Masanosuke's head with all this vicious nonsense about the district office? You are wicked and utterly without scruples. And what's this you're wearing—a woolen *haori*?* Tell me, what makes you think you can act so arrogantly?"

"I have no memory of writing such a letter," I replied. "As for this woolen *haori*, I wear it because if I, with my low stipend, went around in shabby clothes, no one would lend me money. I have no choice."

"Well, I've heard other things about you—that you spend all your time carousing in the Yoshiwara. Most people your age have given up these things. But you are incorrigible."

"I agree you have a point there, but the acquaint-ances I make there are necessary to my livelihood."

My brother became even more furious. "No matter what I say, you talk back. There isn't one relative who talks to me like that. You're the only brazen one. Say another word, and I'll cut you down!" He grasped the handle of his sword.

"Even for you, dear brother," I said, "those are harsh words. May I remind you that I, too, am an honorable retainer of the shogun. We may differ in rank, but as the saying goes, 'dogs and hawks do serve the same master.' You are mistaken if you think you can cut me down just like that." I took hold of my short sword.

*Wool was a luxury item throughout the Tokugawa period.

At this moment Hikoshirō's wife intervened. After calming down the two of us, she took me to her room. She said, "Please settle this matter about Masanosuke."

I went straight to Saburōemon's house and said to him point-blank, "There's not much love lost between us brothers, is there?"

"But I was only thinking of your own good when I told Hikoshirō," he insisted.

I asked to have his head bailiff, Tarōji, come into the room. I told him how Saburōemon had bungled job after job in the past, how he was incapable of managing anything—even his household affairs—and that since he was unfit for his present assignment, the sooner he resigned the better. Tarōji looked puzzled. "Could you explain what you mean by that?"

"What I mean is that my brother can't even tell when something's been written by his own brother or not. So how can you expect him to handle important negotiations as a district administrator?"

Saburōemon reached over for the letter in the official document box and threw it at me angrily. "Look at this and tell me you didn't write it!"

I picked up the letter and asked for a candle. I read it out loud three times and returned it to my brother. "Someone has certainly done a good job of copying my handwriting—"

"So you still refuse to admit it's yours?"

"That's what I mean when I say you're not very smart. If I had written the letter, do you think I would have read it so smoothly and distinctly? Someone who has to deal with a lot of people would have surely known that much—otherwise how is he to carry out an important job? I realize that all the relatives look down on me because I haven't received an appointment. Still, have you ever heard of anyone else who, while at the shogunate court, had the courage to stand up against an undeserved insult? Alas, that I should be so unworthy as to have a brother who cannot distinguish true from false—"

After that speech the two were at a loss for words. At length Saburōemon said, "I apologize. This must be a forgery."

"All right then. Send a note to Hikoshirō explaining everything."

Saburōemon agreed to this, and in a while an answer came from Hikoshirō saying that he was fully satisfied. I got up to leave, but on my way out I noticed that my nephews had lined up in the adjoining room, their short swords at the ready. "Ha ha ha," I laughed. "You should've been prepared like this the day your brother Chūzō was murdered—he might not have been done in so easily. Look at you, all set to attack your uncle. Is there no limit to stupidity?" I heard later that the whole family was enraged over what I had said.

Both of my older brothers kept a close watch on me. I couldn't care less and passed my days carousing to my heart's content.

Saburōemon's son Masanosuke stopped by one day to talk about his father. I had some bills at the brothels, but instead of paying them, I got hold of six *ryō* and invited Masanosuke and one of his father's retainers to the Yoshiwara. Saburōemon made such a fuss when he heard of this that I finally went to see his wife. I cleverly evaded her questions, and the matter was considered closed.

Hikoshirō had heard right, though. For the last three or four years I had fallen into dissolute ways and been spending most of my time in the Yoshiwara. So much so that the roughnecks who prowled through the quarters had become my underlings, and no one dared defy me. Naturally, this took huge amounts of money, but I was determined not to fall into debt, and so I hustled every night at the markets. I just barely stayed ahead.

One day in the summer I was summoned to Hikoshirō's house in Kamezawa-chō. Before leaving I gave my wife instructions concerning the children and the house. At my brother's house everyone was in tears. His wife took me to Shintarō's room and said, "Kokichi, why do you persist in behaving so recklessly? Your brother has made inquiries about you here and there, and worried that you might do something truly dreadful, he's decided to lock you up in a cage. Shintarō and the rest of us tried to talk him out of it, but he wouldn't listen. The cage was finished yesterday—it's in the garden—and your brother was ready to throw you in last night. Shintarō persuaded him not to, but I really don't know what to do. Go take a look at the cage, in any case."

I went out to the garden. The cage was sturdily built with double enclosures. I said to Shintarō and my sister-in-law, "I appreciate my brother's concern. This time, though, may I suggest that you get some candles to light for me, because I've already made up my mind to stay in the cage for good and not come out even if

I'm forgiven. You see, around where I live in Honjo, I'm well known and regarded as a hero of sorts. The fact is that people who don't know me are looked down upon. But after a humiliation like this, I could never show my face to my fellow men. I will fast and die as soon as possible. Yes—I had a feeling that something like this was going to happen, and before coming I told my wife what to do just in case. So, Shintarō, here are my swords. I will do as you wish."

My sister-in-law pleaded with me. "Now that things have come to this, please turn over a new leaf."

"No, it's too late. I won't change my mind."

Shintarō spoke up. "I see what you mean, but I still think you should try—"

"What sense would there be if I did? Ever since my father died I've had no one to turn to, and as for any hope of obtaining office, I gave that up a long time ago. I decided I might as well do what I want and die. Well, I no longer wish to cause my brother trouble, so if I may enter the cage now—"

"I rather thought you would say you'd starve yourself to death," Shintarō said. "I tried my best to catch my father in a good mood and talk him out of it— and now look."

"What matters most is my brother's peace of mind," I assured him. "I really think it would be better if I went in the cage. I had an inkling about this for some time—my friends keep me informed, you know—and I was quite prepared. No, I wasn't surprised one bit."

"Couldn't you at least go home and talk it over with your wife?"

"That won't be necessary. As I said, I'm not at all

worried about my family. Rintarō is sixteen.* He'd be better off if I were dead. If I lived too long, I'd only be a nuisance. But I would be grateful if you would look after him—"

My sister-in-law insisted that I go home for the time being. I went home and waited. At eight I had still received no word, so I took off for the Yoshiwara and stayed for the night.

Shintarō urged me to write a letter of apology to my brother. "He'll have to be appeased one way or another," he said. I couldn't be bothered. Then I heard that my sister-in-law, worried sick, was going from temple to temple asking for prayers on my behalf. I decided to put her mind at rest once and for all. The following spring I passed on the family headship to Rintarō.† I was thirty-seven.

---

*Rintarō was actually fifteen by Japanese count at the time.
†Tenpō 9 (1838).

# Life after Retirement

I now had to earn pocket money. I tore around doing favors for people and racked my brain thinking up money-making schemes. At the same time I was curious to find out what had brought me to this pass. I wondered—who had given Hikoshirō the idea of locking me up in a cage?

I probed around and became fairly certain that Saburōemon and his family had been behind it, peddling tales to Hikoshirō and even feeding him lies, all in revenge for their humiliation the year before. Well, then, I could teach them a lesson, too.

I was aware that Masanosuke had turned out to be a real good-for-nothing and was causing his father no end of worry and distress. I invited him to my home one day and cajoled him into revealing all he knew about his father's machinations. Afterward I made sure that he was well supplied with cash—strictly on loan. I next learned that Saburōemon had paid off his debts to his rice agent in Asakusa. I got hold of my cousin

Takeuchi—he'd retired recently, too—and tricked him into getting a duplicate made of my brother's seal. This done, I sent him with Masanosuke and Suwabe Ryūzō to Saburōemon's rice agent to ask for a loan of 175 *ryō*. "Tell him it's to cover unexpected official expenses at my brother's house."

The rice agent didn't suspect a thing, especially since the three appeared dressed in *kataginu* and *hakama* and bearing a very official-looking box. He handed over the entire sum. I spent it in no time.

The deception came to light two months later. My brother—a real miser—was extremely angry, but no matter how he ranted, I claimed total ignorance. The rice agent made inquiries on his own, but I was never found out.


Suwabe Ryūzō dropped by one day. He said, "There's going to be a three-dice gambling game[41] the day after tomorrow in Tokiwabashi. I'd appreciate it if you'd come with me. About one thousand *ryō* will be at stake, and if I win, I'll have a lot of money and won't feel safe going home alone."

"Sorry, I'm not interested. I've never gambled and don't intend to."

"Come along for the food, then—you can always take a nap."

Suwabe had only thirteen *ryō* to gamble with, ten of which he'd borrowed from me. I said I would go.

Fifty or sixty men, mostly heads of rice broker shops and rich merchants from the Nihonbashi area, had gathered at the teahouse. They began gambling, so after I'd had my fill of the food, I went to a brothel in Tokiwa-chō and called for a woman to pass the time.

A messenger came for me around four in the morning. Back at the teahouse I saw that Suwabe had won about six hundred *ryō*. I persuaded him to quit and walked him home. I remember how amused everyone was when I said it was the first time that I'd ever seen such a game. "Oh, but isn't Master Katsu the well-brought-up fellow," they chuckled.

The gambling game gave me the idea of lending money to friends and acquaintances at high interest. It was a profitable arrangement, as I soon found out. Some of those I lent money to were women who worked at teahouses in the Okuyama section of Asakusa. They took their time in paying me back, but I didn't mind, since everyone in Okuyama bowed and scraped as if I were the boss of the neighborhood.

Among the students in my son's judo class was an older man by the name of Shimada Toranosuke.[42] He was an accomplished swordsman and feared as much for his quick temper as for his skills. I had heard that he had defeated all the students at the Otani school and recently opened his own school in Shinbori in Asakusa. I decided it was time to meet him. I also knew that he had come up from Kyushu two or three years ago, and it was my guess that he wasn't too knowledgeable about the ways of the city of Edo. Why not shake him up a bit, I thought. I wore for the visit an underrobe of bright red crepe, a kimono of decidedly rakish design, and over that a short *haori*. At my side I stuck a wooden sword.

*Nihonbashi*. From *Edo meisho zue*.

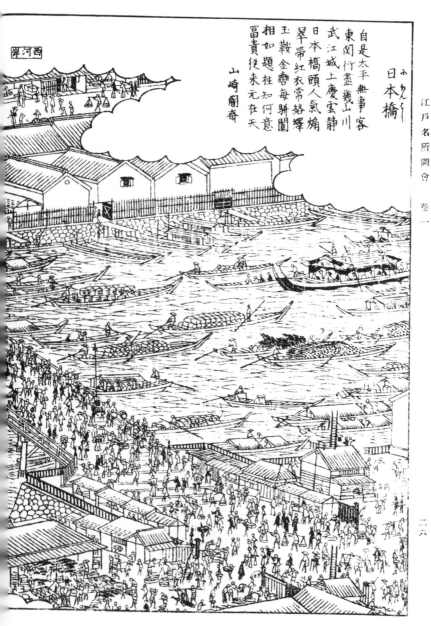

西河岸

日本橋

自是太平無事客
東閣行盡幾山川
武江城上慶雲靜
日本橋頭人氣煙
翠帶紅衣常絡繹
玉鞍金靶每駢闐
相如題柱知何意
富貴從來元在天

山崎闇齋

二六

A student opened the front door of his house and asked who I was.

"Tell your master the retired Katsu is here."

Toranosuke came out at once. He was dressed in a *hakama*. I was shown to the sitting room, and after we'd exchanged the usual courtesies—I thanked him for his kindness to my son—we chatted about swordsmen and the art of fencing in general. Through all this, he kept staring at my getup. It also struck me that just to spite me he was deliberately bringing up the names of the world's known idlers and ne'er-do-wells. He was known to be rather straitlaced, so I let it pass.

It was getting close to four. I said, "This being my first visit, I'd thought of bringing a present, but I wasn't sure of what you liked, so I'm afraid I've come empty-handed. Do you like sake by any chance?"

"No, I don't drink."

"What about good food then?"

"Yes, that I like."

"In that case could I trouble you to come with me to Asakusa?"

He declined, but when I told him I wouldn't take no for an answer, he reluctantly agreed to come. As we walked by the teahouses in Okuyama, I teased and flirted with all the women out in front. Toranosuke trailed behind in open-mouthed amazement.

"Shall we have some sushi?" I asked. He nodded. "Come on then, I'll take you somewhere interesting." I led him toward the Yoshiwara, but when we were about to go through the main gate, he objected. "No thank you, no thank you." I seized him by the arm anyway and dragged him into Okamezushi, an eatery on Nakanochō, the main street. We went to the second floor and ordered sushi.

"Tora, do you smoke?"

"A little, but I've given it up now that I'm in training."

"Hah—that's what I call being fainthearted. Whoever said you can't smoke just because you're in training? Listen, I came to visit you today because I'd heard that you were a really tough guy, but if you're going to be like that, you'll never be able to make your way in this city."

"Well, if you say so, I'll smoke. Just today."

I called down for someone to buy a pipe and tobacco. "Now for some sake," I said. He gave the same excuse, but I made him drink anyway.

By now the sun had set. Lanterns glowed here and there and added to the beauty of the cherry blossoms that had just come out. From our second floor window I pointed out to Tora the courtesans promenading through the narrow streets. He gazed intently at the scene below and sighed, "It certainly is a world apart."

I thought I would give him an idea of my power and influence in the Yoshiwara and took him on a complete tour. I strutted and swaggered, and when I'd decided that he had been sufficiently awed, I led him to the brothel Sanotsuchiya and asked for the best-looking woman in the house. We were told that with the cherry blossoms in season the rooms were all booked, but when I let them know who was speaking, a room was opened up straightaway. We stayed until morning and parted company at Morinoshita.

Toranosuke must have been really impressed because I heard from Matsuura Kanji, a retainer in the service

*Near the Main Gate Leading to the Yoshiwara.* From *Edo meisho zue.*

大門通

むかしこのあたり地ぶ吉原町
ありしゆゑ頃の大
門の通り多く
しのこりかく
今ハ鍋
物屋馬具師
多く住り

翠れんぎ
の玉

of Matsudaira Naiki, that he was telling everyone, "I would never have believed that anyone could get away with that kind of behavior in the Yoshiwara. I wonder how he got to be so popular?" He also was saying, "The retired Katsu will come to no harm in the Yoshiwara." Hikoshirō and his family were much relieved to hear this, I was told. So with nothing better to do, I spent the time amusing myself in Asakusa and the Yoshiwara.

On Toranosuke's suggestion I decided to go on a pilgrimage to Katori and Kashima shrines. I asked Matsuura Kanji to come with me. We left early in the fourth month. Traveling through Shimōsa Province, I took part in fencing matches at practice halls. Many of the teachers had stayed with me at one time or another, so all my expenses were taken care of. At Chōshi my legs started giving me trouble, so I sent Kanji ahead to the places where we were expected and returned to Edo, sleeping comfortably all the way in a big boat.

I became interested in *jōruri** and looked forward each day to my walks in Asakusa and Shitaya listening to street-side chanters. In the sixth month—or was it the end of the fifth—Tora's brother Kinjirō came up from Kyushu. I showed him the sights and went back and forth between the two houses looking after him. He was the kind of person who did everything I said, so I usually had him stay with me.

One evening, on our way to see a *niwaka*† dance in

---

*Narrative chants from the Jōruri puppet theater; they were sung to the accompaniment of the samisen, a stringed instrument.
†A dance performed at a *niwaka kyōgen*, a comic entertainment popular in the Yoshiwara.

the Yoshiwara, I purposely picked a fight at Umamichi. That scared him completely. He claimed to have a reputation in Kyushu as a rowdy, but from what I saw of him, I'd say he was pretty tame. When he left at the end of the eighth month, I saw him off as far as Kawasaki.

Young Magoichirō, my landlord, was getting over his head in debt. A while back when I'd found him a wife, I had fixed things up by cajoling the peasants on his fiefs into covering immediate expenses. He had lately taken to drink, however, and become increasingly careless, thinking nothing of inviting a common townsman into his living quarters to tipple with him. His uncle Sennosuke deceived him at every turn and helped himself to household articles to pay for his amusements. Another kinsman, Kurahashi, duped him into lending an enormous amount of money. And now more recently Magoichirō had moved into his house the daughter of a rice shop owner in the neighborhood and was spending his nights in drunken revelry. His finances were as bad as they had ever been.

Sennosuke suggested to Magoichirō that he hire someone called Ōkawa Jōsuke to oversee his accounts. The men on Magoichirō's fiefs opposed this, as did his father-in-law, Gonnosuke. They asked me to block the move, but when I talked to Magoichirō about it, he became angry and threatened to evict me. I told him off in so many words and made him apologize.

Jōsuke, in the meantime, had slipped five *ryō* to Sennosuke. He was hired as the family overseer. Then, while supposedly setting the household finances in order, he was discovered to have pocketed thirty *ryō*, on the pretext of securing an appointment for his master.

The creditors kept coming, but payment was out of the question. Sennosuke talked Jōsuke into putting up the money. Jōsuke claimed that total expenses came to 339 *ryō*, and handing Magoichirō a household account book—he kept one copy for himself—he asked for reimbursement. Unable to pay, Magoichirō decided to cook up an excuse and fire him.

Jōsuke was much too smart for him. Waiting for a night when Magoichirō was befuddled by drink, he stole his master's account book and burned it. Magoichirō was in a quandary, for without evidence there was no way to tell whether Jōsuke had cheated on the figures. No amount of protesting was of any use.

A month went by. Negotiations with Jōsuke were at a standstill. Magoichirō's relatives felt it was time to step in. Though they tried various arguments, Jōsuke insisted that he be paid in full. The matter was brought to the attention of Okano Dewa-no-kami, the head of the main branch of the family. Okano sent over one of his retainers to bargain with Jōsuke, but short of evidence, there wasn't much he could do either. Another uncle, Soga Matazaemon, came forth. He, too, was powerless. The situation remained at an impasse.

Jōsuke took it into his head to present a petition of grievance to the senior councillor Ōta Bingo-no-kami and ran up to that official's palanquin as he was traveling to Edo Castle. He was promptly handed over to Magoichirō, with orders from his commissioner, Tōyama Aki-no-kami, that he be put under guard.* Jōsuke was locked up in one of the rooms adjoining the outer gate, extra samurai were hired to watch him, and a number of peasants were called in from the nearby fiefs to help out.

Once again Magoichirō's relatives assembled to confront Jōsuke. He wouldn't give in, though, for besides being well read and eloquent, he knew a lot about legal matters and was very confident—altogether too much of a match for anyone. Even the men sent from the commissioner's office had been argued down.

As matters were going from bad to worse, Jōsuke escaped from his room and tried again to petition the senior councillor. Once more he was turned over to Magoichirō. Security was strengthened. Then Jōsuke's wife decided to present a petition of grievance to the senior councillor, and duly intercepted, was placed under guard in a room near the front hall. Amidst this confusion Magoichirō's men were running around trying to borrow money to cover the daily upkeep of the growing household.

The officials from the commissioner's office were replaced by another pair. They were just as easily done in by Jōsuke. "Why," everyone laughed, "it's as though the men are being sent in to be made fun of." Jōsuke's wife escaped and was caught a second time trying to petition the senior councillor. Additional guards had to be mounted, and as if this wasn't bad enough, it was learned that Jōsuke's son, who was in service elsewhere, had also petitioned the senior councillor. He

*The petitioning of a government official on his way to work was a criminal offense.

was brought to the house and put in a room near the inner entrance. There were now three rooms to guard and even higher expenses.

Everyone was at a loss, for there was no prospect of either money or a settlement. The assistant commissioner at Tōyama's office had already resigned pleading illness, and then when one of Tōyama's men went to the senior councillor's office to take custody of Jōsuke's son, he was told, "The senior councillor has been hinting that for someone of his rank and position your superior, Aki-no-kami, is taking an unconscionably long time over what is after all a minor affair concerning one retainer of Okano Magoichirō."

Tōyama withdrew from office the next day, also on the pretext of illness. He was succeeded by Honda Hyūga-no-kami from another unit. Honda sent over his own men to talk to Jōsuke, but they, of course, made no headway. By now Magoichirō's relatives were getting sick of the whole thing.

A friend said to me one day, "Katsu, here you are, living on Magoichirō's land, and all you do is sit back and watch this big to-do. Any reason why?"

"As a matter of fact, yes. All these years I looked after Magoichirō—seeing how he's so incompetent— and made sure that he and his family got enough to eat. But when I warned him not to hire Jōsuke, he threatened to evict me. So I've decided not to worry about him anymore. And that goes for this recent trouble, too."

I passed the time listening to street-side *gidayū*\*

---

\*A variant of *jōruri*.

chanters. I had retired and was entitled to these modest consolations. Magoichirō could go to the devil for all I cared. I purposely stayed away from home and slept every night at Toranosuke's house.

I next heard that even the new commissioner was stumped and thinking of demoting Magoichirō to the *kobushingumi* and leaving it at that. Then, to add to everyone's woes, Jōsuke's son disappeared. This was very serious, for when someone handed over by the senior councillor absconded, the family responsible was usually tried by the shogunate court, and if worse comes to worst, its name dishonored. Jōsuke and his family were elated, while Magoichirō and his family sank deeper into gloom.

Jōsuke's wife chose this moment to give notice that she had run out of breast milk. All on account of not having been given three meals a day she said and delivered her three small children to Magoichirō. A nursemaid and wet nurse had to be found in a hurry, and with so many things happening at once, the new officials in charge threw up their hands and left.

In the evening two officials came from Hyūga-no-kami's office with the message that come what may, the case would be brought to court the next day. All the relatives gathered but could not agree on any solution. I was at home that day entertaining Toranosuke, but even I had to admit that I'd never heard of such a tangle.

Jōsuke took the opportunity to escape once again. He was discovered as he was slipping out the front gate and quickly surrounded. Swords were drawn, and in the confusion Jōsuke's wife eluded the guards. She, too, was caught, restrained, and brought back to the house tied by a rope. When Jōsuke heard what had been done to his wife, he stormed into Magoichirō's front hall and demanded, "Since when has it been permitted to tie up the wife of a samurai?" No one knew how to handle him.

It was at this juncture that Magoichirō's relatives sent a note asking me to come. I declined, saying I had a guest. They kept sending over messages, however, so I excused myself from Toranosuke and went to see Magoichirō and his family. They poured out their woes. "Katsu-san, there must be something you can do."

I said, "I rather thought it would turn out like this. If you recall, I was against hiring Jōsuke from the very beginning. But Magoichirō not only wouldn't listen, he got together with his uncle Sennosuke and tried to throw me out. Oh, I was aware of what was going on," I continued. "No one asked for my opinion, though, so I decided it was none of my business. Well, isn't it a little late to be asking for help? Besides, I'm not sure I could deal with Jōsuke—he's a formidable adversary, as you know by now. Sorry, I can't help you."

As I stood up to leave, Gonnosuke, Magoichirō's father-in-law, pleaded with me to reconsider. I said, "Very well, I will negotiate with Jōsuke, but you'll have to be prepared to reimburse him."

"But that's impossible—"

"It would be useless talking to him then."

I went home. Toranosuke was waiting for me. "Master Katsu," he said. "I know you've helped a great many people in the past. Now this comes up—something so big that not even the commissioner and all the relatives put together can handle it. It's being taken to court tomorrow, and if you merely stand by, all the good you've done will have been in vain. Don't you think you should step forward?"

"I've retired and can do without that sort of trouble."

"That may be so, but just this once couldn't you help?"

"Why don't you go and talk to them then?"

Tora went and came back to tell me that everyone agreed that only I, Katsu Kokichi, could get them out of this disaster. I went over. The relatives entreated me to help them. "We'll leave everything up to you, Katsu-sama." I promised to do what I could and went to talk to the officials on duty.

"Magoichirō and his relatives have asked me to settle this affair," I said. "I have a certain plan in mind. Do you think Hyūga-no-kami would have any objections?"

"Indeed not," they answered. "If you could dispose of this matter, all of us concerned, not to mention Hyūga-no-kami, would be very grateful. Please act as you see fit."

I had all the Okano relatives put their signatures to a sheet of paper. From Magoichirō himself I obtained a set of written statements to the effect that one, he would allow absolutely no one to interfere with my plan, and two, he would leave money and any other pertinent business to my discretion.

That done, I said to everyone, "Now that I have agreed to take care of this matter, let me say that I have no intention of asking for your advice. There is one thing, though, that I would like to make clear.

This mischief by Jōsuke, if you will pardon my saying so, was entirely your own doing. In the first place Jōsuke could not have raised so much money in so short a time. Had he in fact raised it, Magoichirō's finances would have improved. Instead, they've continued to grow worse. I don't know why Magoichirō has not even a single change of clothes, but in general it is because Jōsuke has achieved no results in his job. Personally, I think that Jōsuke's cheated the accounts by taking advantage of the total lack of supervision. But it was Magoichirō who was responsible for the loss of the account book."

"What would you like me to do? Settle the case by reimbursing Jōsuke? Or settle it without paying him a penny? I will do as you wish. If we take the first course, we'll have to pay him in full, and that's a lot of money. Of the two, which do you prefer?"

The relatives held a consultation. "Let's reimburse him in full and consider the case closed," they said.

"That would be easier in a way. Yet I somehow hesitate to hand over money that's been obtained dishonestly."

"Well, how do you propose to settle it without paying him?"

"I can't tell you. Remember, it was because you were such cowards that Jōsuke made fools of you. If I told you now what I intend to do, you'd all faint dead away."

Everyone looked mystified.

I continued. "I'll go talk to Jōsuke while you are still here and convince him that his family should stay in the same room with him. This should make things easier for the guards and give them a good night's rest.

Well, for now, why don't you forget your worries and have something to drink?"

I had some sake brought from my home and while everyone was drinking, I talked to Jōsuke and got him to agree to let his family join him. The relatives and the officials thanked me repeatedly and left. Magoichirō and his family were so worn out by the events of the past months that they slept until late the next day.

I had another long talk with Jōsuke and promised him that he would be repaid in full by the nineteenth day of the twelfth month. To see him through till then I gave him fifteen *ryō* and said I would arrange for him to receive his stipend as usual. We exchanged notes to that effect, and after the negotiations had been concluded without a hitch, I took off the next day for some rest and amusement. In the evening I went to Magoichirō's house. His family greeted me with smiles and made a big fuss.

The money had to be raised, but I knew that as long as I stayed in Edo I wouldn't get a penny. I would have to go to Magoichirō's fief in Settsu Province.* There was also more pressing business at hand. Magoichirō had spent so much over the Jōsuke affair that he could scarcely pay his daily help. Even worse, he said, he had anywhere from thirty to forty mouths to feed and less than a day's worth of rice in the house.

I summoned the peasants from his fief in nearby Musashi and told them to put up the money to cover household expenses until the twelfth month. They refused at first, but when I explained the situation, they

*Now part of Osaka Prefecture.

grudgingly consented. I then persuaded Jizaemon, a village headman in the fief, to lend me forty *ryō* for my travel expenses to Settsu and said I'd return it by the end of the year.

Earlier in the seventh month I had submitted a request to my commissioner to become a lay Buddhist priest and change my name. I received permission from Waki-saka Nakatsukasa Shōyū on the seventeenth day of the tenth month. I took the religious name of Musui, but as my shaved samurai hairdo had not yet grown in, I decided to travel under my samurai name as a retainer of Okano Magoichirō.

I asked Toranosuke to tend to my affairs in my absence. On the ninth day of the eleventh month I set off on the Nakasendō post road.* Accompanying me were Hotta Kisaburō, Iyama Yūhachi, and two other men.

At the post station in Kumagaya, Jizaemon was wait-ing for me with the forty *ryō*. I was feeling none too well, but I pushed my men to cover as much distance as possible. We arrived at last at the Hakken'ya† in Osaka. We rested for several days and then went to Sonezaki, to the north of the city, to call on a friend, Kagatora. He was fortunately at home, and when I explained to him the purpose of my trip, he readily agreed to my request for a loan.

We arrived the next day at the village of Goganzuka,

---

*The post road connecting Edo and Kusatsu, a town just east of Kyoto; it was more circuitous and less traveled than the Tōkaidō.
†Landing place for boats on the Yodo River; it had accommodations for travelers.

Magoichirō's fief in Settsu. It was about six miles from Osaka. We were put up at the residence of Yamada Shin'uemon, the manager of the fief. I lost no time in filling him in about the details of the situation in Edo. In the morning I called together the villagers and told them of the urgent need for money. Shin'uemon said, "As you know, the rice yield of the village is assessed at five hundred *koku*, and the villagers have already lent over seven hundred *ryō*. I doubt if they can put up another penny." I had been told by Magoichirō and his retainers that the amount lent by the village came to five hundred *ryō* and had undertaken the trip on that assumption. This huge discrepancy was a complete surprise. I was extremely annoyed but said nothing and dismissed the villagers for the day. If I set my mind to it, I knew there would always be a way.

I spent the next few days walking around the village. The villagers seemed relatively prosperous[43]—a good sign. I asked Shin'uemon how much it cost the villagers to accommodate official visitors. He replied that whenever a retainer came on business, he usually came with only one man, and daily expenses amounted to eighteen silver *monme*. There were five of us. We would have to be very frugal.

I told my men to decline all side dishes and to take them instead to Shin'uemon's mother. Each day I reminded them how important it was to cut down on expenses, though now and then I slipped them some money to sneak off to Itami for food and drink. Within several days, looking very pleased, Shin'uemon reported that our daily upkeep came to only ten *monme*. I refrained from bringing up the subject of money and took trips to Osaka for my own diversion as well as to gather information on the sly about the villagers. The rumor was that they had no intention of putting up the money. "They're simply waiting for you to get so bored that you'll leave," someone said.

To pass the time, every evening I invited Shin'uemon and the villagers and their children to hear me tell stories about the exploits of famous generals and brave warriors. They were very much taken and listened absorbed until late at night.

One day I again raised the subject of money. The villagers protested, "But we don't have any money." I dropped the matter. It then came to light that my man Iyama Yūhachi had on his own been pressuring the villagers to put up money. Feelings ran high. The angry villagers met day after day for discussions and began milling around our living quarters waving bamboo spears and shouting abuses. My men were afraid and said they wanted to go back to Edo. I gave them a piece of my mind.

The villagers continued to hold their daily meetings, rushing to the local temple at the sound of the bell. And all because of Iyama's stupid demands.

I wasn't a bit fazed. Now and then I put on my kimono with the shogunal crest* and marched around the village with a retainer in tow. This never failed to send the villagers scurrying. Every morning I had Hotta Kisaburō give readings on the *Greater Learning* and the *Book of Filial Piety* and invited Shin'uemon and his

*Presumably the kimono given to Katsu's adoptive father on the occasion of an audience with the shogun in 1792.

family to join us. Shin'uemon, a well-meaning and upright soul, appreciated this and offered to negotiate with the villagers on his own. I said no. For I had a plan up my sleeve—something so startling that the villagers would hand over the money even while foaming at the mouth. I bided my time.

I came down with scabies and commuted daily to Koyama Hot Springs in Itami. But I set a man to spy on developments in the village. He found out that the village officials were cooking up various evil plots. I pretended not to know.

We had been in Goganzuka for some time. I thought I would pay a visit to Shimoyama Yauemon, a friend who was in the service of Hori Iga-no-kami, the magistrate of Osaka. I had done several favors for him back in Edo and was sure I could count on him. I talked to him in private—he already knew all about Magoichirō and his troubles—and returned to Goganzuka.

Shin'uemon was curious about my trip. "May I ask who you visited in Osaka?" he asked.

"Oh, Iga-no-kami, the magistrate—we used to take fencing lessons together."

"You don't say!" He looked intimidated.

Several days later a messenger arrived from Osaka with a train of bearers. He delivered an oral communication from the magistrate and presented me with boxes filled with fish and other delicacies. The villagers were struck dumb. "Little did we know, Katsu-sama, that you were friends with the Osaka magistrate." They put away their bamboo spears and gave up surrounding our lodgings. It was really funny.

I distributed the fish to the village officials and gave

the rest to Shin'uemon and his family. It was reported that they all ate the food reverently, bowing their heads and murmuring, "A gift, a precious gift from the magistrate himself." They were also apparently chastened and willing to talk about money. I could carry out my scheme any day.

One morning I announced to Shin'uemon that I wished to make a pilgrimage to Nose Myōken Shrine and that I would be taking with me my man Kisaburō and two or three of the villagers who had been particularly troublesome. I wore the kimono with the shogunal crest and took along a spear box.* I said to the group, "Today I go not as a retainer of Okano Magoichirō but as a pilgrim." Just before leaving I said to Shin'uemon, "Could you get me a complete set of rainwear?"

"Oh, that won't be necessary," he said. "The weather's been fine for the past few days, and I'm sure it won't rain for at least five or six days."

"Then let me tell you that I've been devoted to Myōken-sama for many years and that every time I pray, it pours. So get some rainwear, will you?" He grudgingly provided a porter to carry the rainwear.

We set off, stopping at Ikeda long enough for the porter to go back and fetch a covering for my palanquin. The weather remained clear, and as we climbed uphill toward Mount Nose, we could see in the distance Osaka, Amagasaki, and further down the coastline of Settsu. For winter it was unusually warm, and even with only one layer of clothing, we perspired. No one

*Part of the equipment for a daimyo procession; Katsu took it to lend an air of formality to the trip.

imagined for a moment that it would rain. The porter grumbled and complained.

I left my palanquin at a teahouse at the foot of Mount Nose and walked the last stretch to the peak. We purified ourselves with water from the shrine well and climbed the flight of steps leading to the main prayer hall. The other worshippers scattered in all directions when they saw the crest on my kimono, and we were left to pray undisturbed.

We took refreshments in the teahouse outside the main gate and began our descent. Halfway down I saw banks of rain clouds drifting over from Mount Rokkō in Arima.

"You're in luck," I said to the porter. "Any moment now it'll rain and your load will be lighter."

Everyone disagreed. "Just because there are rain clouds, it doesn't mean it's going to rain."

"I wouldn't want it to rain before we got to the inn anyway," I said, but urged them, nevertheless, to hurry.

No sooner had we reached the foot of the mountain than it began to pour. There was still some distance to the inn. The men were drenched, but I was nice and dry in the palanquin.

It stormed through the night and let up only around four in the morning. I stayed awake, warming myself at the hearth—you could never tell what the villagers might do, though there was no question that they had been impressed. "Katsu-sama," they said. "You are a man of truly strange and wondrous powers. You knew all along it was going to rain. It can mean only one thing—that the gods pay special attention to your prayers. Yes, indeed, the honorable bannermen of the shogun are really different. The likes of us could pray for a hundred days, and this would never happen." I thought to myself, "I've got them now."

We made a brief detour to the Tada Gongen Shrine and arrived back at Goganzuka about four. That night Iyama came stealthily to my bedside. He said, "Katsu-san, the whole village is agog about the rain. I have a feeling they've had a change of heart and that you'll be getting the money after all." I was heartened.

The next evening I had Iyama scout the situation again. He reported that the villagers were divided in two—those willing to put up the money and those who were not. Leaving Hotta Kisaburō in charge, I decided to make another trip to Osaka and left early in the morning. I took in a play at Nipponbashi, had another talk with Shimoyama, and stayed overnight at the Hakken'ya.

The following day once again a messenger came from the Osaka magistrate with a letter and gifts of food. I had the food cooked and invited Shin'uemon, his staff, and the village headman. When we had finished eating, I read aloud the letter from the magistrate. Everyone looked subdued.

"Now about the money—" I began.

"We are doing our very best, but so far it's been impossible," they said. I left it at that and went to sleep.

In the morning I called for Shin'uemon. "Today I have a special reason for celebrating, and I would like to invite all the village officials for some sake around four. Order some particularly tasty dishes from Amagasaki—I'll pay for it—and see to it that the soup and all the other dishes are prepared with extra care." I gave him a copy of the menu I had planned and asked to have water heated for a bath. I had Kisaburō fix my hair and bathed while the men cleaned up the sitting room.

Then, leaving word that we were going to Gozu Tennō Shrine in Itami, I took my men to a kimono shop in Itami called the Shirokoya. I ordered three sets of ceremonial robes in linen and two sets of white *haori* and kimono dyed with the Okano family crest. "And have them ready by two this afternoon." The shop-keeper said he would, as long as he didn't have to dye in the crest. I paid for the goods and told him that someone would be by to pick them up.

On the way back I gave my men the particulars of the big farce I proposed to put on that evening. We returned to the village sometime past noon.

I had Kisaburō arrange a few sprays of white camel-lias in a vase to place in the alcove. It was close to five by the time we had attended to all the details. The food was ready to be served and the village officials had gathered in Shin'uemon's office. I asked everyone to come into the sitting room.

"As you've no doubt heard, I have a special reason for inviting you here today. It was good of you to come. Now if you would just make yourselves at home and drink—" I poured sake for everyone. "And if there's anyone here with a hidden talent, please feel free to perform."

I started off with a popular ditty I had picked up during my wilder days in the Yoshiwara. I kept replenishing their cups and urged them to relax and forget formalities of rank. Unlike previous meetings at which money had been mentioned, the villagers were in high spirits, laughing and singing and saying the first thing that popped into their heads. Having satisfied myself that the sake had taken its effect, I ordered tea and rice to conclude the meal. The villagers finished eating, thanked me, and rose to leave.

I hurried out to the garden and washed myself with the buckets of water that had been set out according to plan. I quickly changed into one of the white kimono and wore over it the kimono with the shogunal crest. I piled several cushions in the center of the room, flanked them with a pair of candlesticks, and sat down.

"Kisaburō," I called out. "Tell Shin'uemon and the village officials to come back. I have something important to say."

The villagers demurred. "Couldn't we wait until tomorrow? We've all had too much to drink—"

"No, I can't. I have a previous commitment to go to Osaka tomorrow and will probably be away four or five days. Since you're here anyway, you might as well sober up and listen to this message from your lord and master in Edo."

They straggled back to the adjoining room, and when everyone had been seated, Kisaburō threw open the partitions. The villagers bowed low.

"What I have to say is no less than this," I began. "For the past month all of you have conspired to ignore the repeated request from your lord for funds to settle the Jōsuke affair. It is inexcusable that you should think only of yourselves and look the other way when your lord makes an appeal. Be that as it may, be informed that I herewith call off all talk of money."

The villagers looked grateful and relieved. I went on. "I'll have you know that I made this trip expressly at the request of your lord and at great risk to my health. Time and again I appealed to you for help, but you turned a deaf ear, as if I were just another ordinary retainer. It was the height of rudeness. And then, for reasons I fail to understand, you threatened me and my men with bamboo spears. Pray tell me why you did this. Depending on your answer, I may have to take it up with the Osaka magistrate tomorrow and request a hearing."

Everyone remained huddled on the floor speechless. At length one of them spoke up in tears. "We are entirely to blame. Please have pity and forgive us."

"If you insist—what are you but poor benighted peasants?"

I turned to Shin'uemon. "Since they seem to be genuinely sorry, I will forgive them. There is one request, however, that I would like to make to you and the villagers. You will grant me this, I hope—"

The villagers said, "Anything, anything that we can possibly do. After all, you were good enough to over-look our offenses."

"My request is none other than this. As you know by now, the affair in Edo has involved Magoichirō's relatives, the senior councillor Ōta Bingo-no-kami, and several other high government officials. The fact is, it's much more serious than you imagine. Jōsuke is bar-gaining for all he's worth, nothing's been resolved, and the case threatens to be brought to the shogunate court any day. I, Kokichi, could not stand by idly, but try as I might, without money there was really nothing I could do. And that is why I came to you.

"I realize the amount Magoichirō wants to borrow is enormous and puts you in a difficult position. It isn't that I don't understand your reasons for refusing. All the same, you would do well to remember the debt you owe your lord from the time of his father, Gōsetsu. Indeed, it goes back several generations. Would it be right to forget it? In my opinion to abandon your lord when his family name and honor are in danger is behavior unworthy of even beast or fowl.

"Oh, one or two thousand *ryō* I could have easily borrowed from the Osaka magistrate. But what would be the point then of having been entrusted with the land by Gōsetsu? Just think if it were known that Magoichirō had bypassed his own fief and borrowed from another to restore his family fortune. In the first place it would be most unfilial to his ancestors. Or supposing it were bruited about that he had done this because he couldn't control the peasants on his own land—he would be hard put to revive his family name, much less show his face to his friends and peers.

"I came to Osaka in the hope that you would come forward—that lord and follower together would put things right and set an example of devotion that no one could criticize. But I, Kokichi, failed to raise the money, and having accomplished nothing, I cannot go back to Edo. In atonement I have decided to commit harakiri tonight. My request is simply this—that all of you here see to it that my corpse is delivered by the appropriate officials to my son in Edo. Yūhachi will take this letter immediately to Magoichirō. Kisaburō has already agreed to administer the final blow with his sword* and explain everything to my wife and children when he returns to Edo. As for the other two who accompanied me here from Edo, I thank them for all they've done. They may keep whatever money I gave them and leave tomorrow or do as they wish. I have nothing further to say. Ah yes, this kimono from the shogun—I leave with the village officials. Treat it with respect."

I took off my kimono and put it on a large tray. Handing Kisaburō my long sword, I said, "Use this to cut off my head." I ordered one of my men to bring the container in which to place my decapitated head— I'd brought it from Edo—and as I unsheathed my dagger and wound its handle with a strip of cloth, I reminded everyone to carry out my instructions. I looked around the room. "You may raise your heads now. Behold how Katsu Kokichi commits harakiri!" I held up the dagger.

"Stop. Please stop!" Crying out, the villagers crawled toward me.

"Kisaburō, are you ready?"

He remained bowed to the floor.

"Must I ask someone else?"

Kisaburō slowly got up and went behind me. Several villagers clung to him and wailed. "Please wait—we have something to say."

*In ritual harakiri another man stood by to administer the final blow by decapitation.

"Quickly then," Kisaburō said.

"Katsu-sama, we'll do whatever you say. Yes, even if we have to sell our possessions."

I said, "It's too late now."

"Please—we beg of you not to take your life. Please."

They beseeched me weeping and sobbing. I returned the dagger to its scabbard.

Shin'uemon tottered forward on his knees in a daze. "It is all my fault for not discharging my duties as manager of the fief. At the very least please cut off my head and send it to Edo."

"That won't be necessary. The blame lies with everyone for being selfish and wanting in respect for their master. As far as I'm concerned, I've retired and don't ask much of this world. It doesn't matter what happens to me, though I was hoping that I might help a lot of people and that even Jōsuke might come round once he heard of my death. But since you insist, I will not take my life. Instead, I will ask you to sign a pledge that you will furnish the money."

The villagers drew up a note immediately and signed their names. "When would you like to have the money?"

"By ten in the morning."

"Yes, yes, anything you say."

As they shuffled out of the room, Kisaburō spoke to them in a stern voice. "Be sure you get the money, because if anything goes wrong, then I'll commit hara-kiri."

The money was collected in a frenzy and presented on a tray the next morning at ten—all of 550 *ryō*, with a promise to have the remaining 50 *ryō* delivered to the House of Shimaya in Edo before we ourselves had returned.[44] The villagers asked that their contribution to Magoichirō's living expenses be reduced from 330 *ryō* to 200 for the coming year. I told them that it was out of the question.

"Would you grant us this request, then?" they said. "Your man Iyama Yūhachi has extorted close to 400 *ryō* over the past year. We would appreciate it if you would hand him over to us so that we can hold an inquiry." I said, "As soon as the work's done." I could see Yūhachi shaking with fright, so after they had left, I told him not to worry.

The next order of business was to punish the villagers. I demoted the village officials who had been particularly defiant to the status of plain water-drinking peasants and replaced them with men who had served in Gōsetsu's time. To those who had lent money, I granted the privilege of bearing surnames, and to Shin'uemon, I gave a set of ceremonial robes, a house, and a plot of land with a yield of almost one *koku* of rice.

By evening all the business had been completed. I told Shin'uemon that my men and I would be going to Kyoto for some sightseeing the next day. "Send some coolies ahead to make the necessary arrangements, and have everything we brought from Edo packed and ready. I'll be needing Yūhachi for a while yet, but I'll send him back from Kyoto." I turned to Yūhachi and said, "You're coming with me, do you hear?"

That night we were chatting and taking our ease when we were told that two village officials, Uichi and Gen'uemon, had come with a written petition claiming they had a note from Magoichirō promising to repay 150 *ryō* by the end of the year. "Tell them to extend the deadline to the coming year," I told Shin'uemon.

I could hear the two protesting in the next room, so I went in and demanded to see the petition. Pretending to read it, I held the paper up to the candle and burned it. Uichi and Gen'uemon blanched and muttered something under their breath.

"Are you criticizing me?" I shouted. "It has come to my attention that you two have been the worst of the lot. I've tolerated it so far, but this time—" They both cringed. "And this note—I'll keep it, thank you." I snatched the document and walked out. With one phrase I had disposed of a debt of 150 *ryō*. I thought then how important it was in life to strike at the right moment.

We left for Kyoto at four in the morning. The villagers didn't say a word. We rested up for three days at an inn near Sanjō Bridge and then set off for the Tōkaidō. During the stop at Ōiso, I had my hair trimmed and combed back to fall behind the ears. At Kawasaki, I sent word ahead that we were returning. A crowd was waiting for us in Edo. It was the ninth day of the twelfth month.

I went straight to Magoichirō's house with the money. The entire family came out and talked as if I were a living god. Two days later I summoned Jōsuke and handed him 339 *ryō*, obtained a receipt that included the signatures of his relatives, and gave it to Magoichirō.[45]

My adoptive grandmother died the next day. I made arrangements for her funeral.

The peasants on Magoichirō's fiefs in Musashi and

Sagami had said that I'd be lucky if I came back with one hundred *ryō*. They were amazed, and as for Mago-ichirō's relative who'd said he would resign from office if I got as much as fifty—well, I guess I put him in his place. My friend Toranosuke was very pleased. Jōsuke himself couldn't have been happier. "Katsu-sama," he said, "as long as I live, I won't sleep with my toes pointed in your direction."* He stops by my house even now.

Only a few days remained until the end of the year. I dashed around settling Magoichirō's affairs. His grateful family invited me to dinner, saying, "It's really the first time since Magoichirō became family head that we've had such a pleasant year's end."

All the people involved in the affair were in awe of me. The truth was, I'd never worked so hard to raise money. The expenses for the trip came to sixty-seven or sixty-eight *ryō*—I'd treated my men to palanquins for the trip back—and though Magoichirō offered me the remainder of the money, I declined. I knew that he had barely enough to see him through the year. My friends also said I should take at least one hundred *ryō*, but I had my own reasons for refusing. I finally accepted a bolt of cotton cloth from the Okano family.

The mourning period for my grandmother was completed early in the new year. I gave myself up to fun and pleasure as it if were my business and flitted about from place to place. If I ran short of pocket money, I could always sell swords for people or come up with one scheme or another.

In time my commissioner got wind of my unau-

---

*A common figure of speech for showing respect and gratitude.

thorized trip to Settsu. He ordered me into domiciliary confinement. It was awfully oppressive, staying home from the second month to the beginning of the ninth, but at least I talked Magoichirō into giving me a monthly allowance of one and a half *ryō* and a bale and a half of rice for the duration of my confinement. I consoled myself pottering about in the garden.

Early in the ninth month a friend went to see the commissioner and explained that my trip to Settsu had not been for pleasure but to help out Magoichirō. The commissioner said, "Katsu went out of necessity, you say? He still shouldn't have crossed a barrier station without permission. But since he seems to be behaving—" He ordered me released from house arrest. After being cooped up for so long, it certainly felt good to gad about again.

I had a second floor built onto the house, and having become interested in the tea ceremony, I added a small tearoom. With my cousin Takeuchi, I browsed through the shops for tea utensils. But greed hath no limits, as they say, and the more I saw the more I wanted. I ran out of money and borrowed from the brothels in the area at agreed-upon rates. I collected twenty-six *ryō* in three days and promptly spent it all on tea utensils. I could think of nothing else, and whenever I was short of cash, I went to the brothels. In all I must have borrowed seventy or eighty *ryō*.

I now got about twenty of the men who hung about the retainers' quarters in Magoichirō's house to work for me free. I had them patrol the brothels in the vicinity and dispatched a man whenever a customer got out of hand. In return the proprietors sent over gifts of cash on the five major feast days of the year.[46] At year's end and at the midsummer Bon festival, too, I received one-half *ryō* from each brothel—a total of seven and a half *ryō*. Four other establishments sent over two *ryō* every year, so that all told I must have made fifty or sixty *ryō* a year. My men, moreover, were given a half *ryō* or so each time they went to the rescue of a teahouse owner who sent for help. For that matter it had gotten so that anyone who wanted to set up shop or conduct business in the area felt obliged to send me "gift money." It was all very simple—I was the boss of the entire neighborhood.

I spent money as though it bubbled right out of the ground. The following year in the second month I started feeling poorly.* I became gravely ill. I went through several treatments and was up and about by the end of the eighth month. But I ran around recklessly too soon and was seriously ill again early in the twelfth month. My body was swollen all over—it hurt even to turn over in bed.

The commissioner must have heard about my high-handed ways. On the twenty-second day of the twelfth month, he ordered me into domiciliary confinement at the Toranomon residence of Hoshina Eijirō, a samurai under the same commissioner as my son. Too weak to walk, I had to go by palanquin. It was only the summer after that I finally recovered.

I tried to retrieve money and items that I had lent

*Tenpō 12 (1841).

to various people in my Honjo neighborhood. The total owed me came to about forty *ryō*, but no one paid up. I had gone to Hoshina's place at a minute's notice and never bothered to make any provisions. There was little I could do, and besides, I had nobody but myself to blame for my poverty.

# Some Other Incidents

It was before I retired. Thinking it would be a good idea to donate a sacred mirror to the Myōken Shrine in Kita Warigesui, I talked to the members of the shrine association. We decided to raise twelve *ryō*.

Among the daily visitors to the shrine was a fine-looking samurai by the name of Nakamura Tachū, who said he was an official in charge of finances for the daimyo of Wakayama. When we told him of our plan to donate a mirror, he said, "Most admirable. Allow me to be a sponsor too." He promised to donate three *ryō*. The rest of us were delighted and fluttered around him saying, "Tachū-sama, we are so beholden to you."

The money was raised, and though I was asked to hold onto it, I was unwilling, and it was handed over to Tachū for safekeeping. That night he disappeared—money and all. We searched everywhere but couldn't find a clue.

I mentioned the incident to Takeuchi Heiuemon

one day. "That fellow Tachū," he said with a laugh, "is what is known as a confidence man."

"And what is that?"

"Well, a confidence man ordinarily dresses in fine clothes and goes around visiting places like shrines and temples and lecture halls where pilgrims are bound to congregate. He wants to impress people, so he pretends to be very devout. He also lets it be known that he handles money for temples and monasteries and the like. Before you know it, he's duped people into giving him money—fees for arranging loans, for instance. Then he moves out of his lodgings and goes elsewhere to practice his tricks.

"It's a regular year-round business, you know," he continued. "Ten or twenty of them work as a group. They bribe the local policeman and his assistants, and they're all set. And if one of their men gets caught and things get sticky, they band together and bail him out one way or another. Yes—your so-called friend Tachū was a confidence man all right. Some of them even work on the highways and fob off quack medicine and such stuff to unsuspecting country folk. But those, I'd call second-class confidence men."

A similar incident took place when I was living on Okano's property. Seven or eight bannermen of my acquaintance in Honjo had heard that the Zōjōji temple in Shiba lent out money. In their eagerness to borrow funds, they were tricked into handing over money to a man who said he'd arrange for a loan. As a result, one of my friends, Hasegawa Kanjirō, was left in considerable financial distress. I had heard enough from Takeuchi to know that this was all part of a confidence game. So I got hold of the culprit—his name was Ishikawa Gorō—and made him return the money.

Another friend, Katsuta Yōgen, was also talked into paying a fee for a loan by a certain Fujisawa Jizaemon. He had no idea where Fujisawa lived, but I tracked him down and recovered the money.

My friend Hasegawa Kanjirō was swindled yet a second time. He met a man called Saitō Kanbutsu to discuss the matter of a loan. Saitō came to see him several days later, and Hasegawa, anxious for a loan, plied him with food and drink. In the course of the visit Saitō brought out a nugget of silver. Hasegawa was quite taken by it and went around the house showing it to his family. He returned to the sitting room, placed the nugget beside him, and resumed his drinking.

When the time came to leave, Saitō asked for the nugget. The two searched the room but could not find it. Saitō left only after Hasegawa had promised to look for it more carefully. Hasegawa looked all over the house but it was nowhere to be seen.

Saitō returned in a few days. He said, "I should tell you that the silver nugget I brought the other day was discovered in a mine in the Wakayama domain. It's already been shown to the daimyo—I was just holding it temporarily. It would be terrible if it were lost." He fooled Hasegawa into giving him five *ryō* and told him, moreover, that he couldn't possibly arrange any loans. Hasegawa and his family were left in a sorry plight.

Imai Sanjirō of Hayashi-chō was a good friend I had taken riding lessons with. He was also tricked by Saitō. In his case he'd been told that he would get a loan from Kōyasan, the temple in Wakayama, and had handed over to Saitō one and a half *ryō* as an "advance gift" for an agent at the temple office in Edo. He never laid eyes on Saitō again.

Imai told me this story after I had told him how Hasegawa had been duped.

"It's the same man, all right," he exclaimed.

"Do you know where this Saitō lives?"

"In the compound of the Nichion'in temple in Asakusa."

"I'll get the money back for you—"

"I doubt if you can—I've already had a policeman look into it."

"Just wait and see, I'll get the money."

We left it at that.

Several days later I went to Saitō's lodgings in Asakusa. An attendant ushered me into the sitting room. I could tell at a glance that Saitō lived in grand style. On the floor was a bearskin rug the size of three tatami mats and against the wall, an imposing Shintō shrine. A rack held a pair of swords with scabbards wrought in gold, and further off in the corner was a stack of wicker hampers and containers for traveling.

Saitō walked in, fingering a rosary of crystal and amber with a sanctimonious air. He had on a *hakama* and a padded *haori* of black silk crepe. I introduced myself, and after we'd talked about devotions and prayers and so on, I mentioned that Nakamura Tachū and I were good friends. I said with a straight face, "He told me about you some time ago, and I'd been meaning to call, but you know, with this and that—" Saitō turned red and quickly whispered something in the attendant's ear. Minutes later the attendant returned with a tray laden with food and sake.

Taking only a sip now and then, I brought up the subject of confidence men. "I always used to ask Tachū to do favors for me, but come to think of it, I haven't seen him since that big flap about the mirror for the Myōken Shrine."

"I believe he's in Shimōsa now."

"So that's it. Well, judging from the splendid furnishings in your house, I'd say you haven't done too badly yourself. What's your line of work, by the way?"

Saitō admitted at last that he was a confidence man. "And Katsu-san, if I could be of some use to you—"

I leaped at the chance to remind him about Imai, got the money, and left.

Imai was very grateful. I said to him, "You've got to deal with these men on their own level. Money's their business, and if you're open with them, they'll be open with you."

In a day or so Saitō came to see me with an attendant carrying gifts. I had him do some work for me, and as a result I got to know quite a bit about the crooked ways of the world. I told Hasegawa one day all about Saitō and his confidence game. He looked very alarmed. But if samurai insist on walking around with their noses stuck up in the air, they'll never learn what's what in this world.

It was when I was still living on Yamaguchi's property. I became hopelessly smitten with a certain woman. In desperation I told my wife about it.

"Leave everything to me," she said. "I'll get her for you."

"Oh, would you—"

"But first you must give me some time off."

"What ever for?"

"I intend to go to the woman's house and persuade her family one way or another to give her to you. You say they're samurai, too, so they could very well try to put me off. Don't worry, I'll get her for you even if I have to kill myself."

I handed my wife a dagger.

She said, "I'll go tonight and bring her back without fail."

I took off for the day looking for something to do and ran into Tonomura Nanpei. As we stood chatting, he said to me, "Katsu-san, I'll bet you're prone to woman trouble—I can tell by the features on your face. Can you think of any particular problem of that nature?"

I told him about the conversation I'd had with my wife earlier on.

"How very commendable of her," he said and went on his way.

I decided to drop by to see my friend Sekikawa Sanuki, a fortune teller. He took one look at me and said, "Something dreadful's about to happen. Come in and we'll talk about it." Inside, Sanuki went on to say that he could see right away that I was having woman trouble. "And this very night I foresee trouble over a sword. A lot of people may be hurt. Tell me, can you think of anything along these lines?" I told him about my infatuation with a woman and my wife's determination to get her for me. He was speechless at first but then started to give me counsel, saying how fortunate I was to have such a devoted wife and how I should take better care of her in the future. I thought about it for a moment. He was right. I was clearly in the wrong. I flew home.

My wife was just about to leave—she had sent her grandmother with our baby daughter to Hikoshirō's in Kamezawa-chō and had finished writing me a note. It took a lot of talking to convince her to give up the idea, but the incident ended without mishap. It wasn't the first time she got me out of trouble.

After that I tried to be more gentle and considerate to my wife. Until then not a day had passed without my hitting her for one reason or another.

Maybe it's because of these past beatings, but she's suddenly become sickly over the last four or five years. I know what—from now on I'll treat her like the retired lady of the house!

A year before my retirement a great fire had ravaged the Yoshiwara, and many of the pleasure houses had been forced to move to temporary quarters.* One day at the Sanotsuchiya—it had been relocated to Yamanoyado—I got into a big fight with Kuma, the son of an employee at the copper mint in Hashiba. We were on the second floor, so I picked up Kuma and threw him down the stairs. He had to be carried home by some men who came running from the mint.

In a while about thirty men appeared with hooked spears. They began surrounding the house. I flung off

*Tenpō 8 (1837).

my outer garments, hitched up the hem of my kimono, and rushed outside swinging my sword. I forced the men to retreat two or three hundred yards, but just then a band of men arrived from the local patrol office to break up the fight.

After this even the crones and shrews who were hired to escort customers to the brothels drew away as soon as they saw me. The brothels in Yamanoyado closed shop for three days, and the incident ended quietly. I was also in a great many other fights, but I've forgotten most of them.

The sword I used that time in Yamanoyado was two feet four inches. In another fight—I'd gone with Tarao Shichirōsaburō, Otani Chūjirō, and several others to the Asakusa fair—I had with me the sword made by Seki no Kane . . .* It was two feet seven inches long and had a leather loop at the tip of the scabbard.

Tarao had asked me at the last minute, and I'd had no time to put on my *hakama*. In the crush of people going through the Kaminarimon gate, my sword got caught in the folds of my kimono. Unable to move my legs, I was carried forward willy-nilly by the crowd.

Out of the blue a man hit Tarao on the head with a big wooden pestle. A samurai, no less. Even while jostled by the crowd, I tried to hold the fellow back by his *haori*, but he hit me on the shoulder with the pestle. Then when I tried to draw my sword, the tip of the scabbard got caught. "Just wait—I'll cut you to pieces!" I roared. The people around me shied away, so I whipped out my sword and struck at the samurai.

*Probably Seki no Kanetoshi. A character on the page of the original manuscript has been eaten by insects.

The blade grazed his back in a straight line, slashing his obi and making his pouch and pair of swords fall out. He ran off without stopping to pick up his belongings.

A man from the guard station at Denbōin came with a long stick. I waved my sword in his face a couple of times and sent the passersby flying. I scooped up the swords and pouch and threw them into the guard station. My friends and I headed immediately for Okuyama.

I had to admit that in a crowd a long sword had its drawbacks—the blade must have barely skimmed the samurai. Tarao got a nasty cut right on his bald head, too. We picked fights along the way and went as far as Ryōgoku Bridge. That evening, with nothing special to do, I went home.

There were scores of other adventures, but they took place so long ago I have all but forgotten them.

# Reflections on My Life

Although I indulged in every manner of folly and nonsense in my lifetime, Heaven seems not to have punished me as yet. Here I am, forty-two, sound of health and without a scratch on my body. Some of my friends were beaten to death; others vanished without a trace or suffered one fate or another. I must have been born under a lucky star, the way I did whatever I pleased. No other samurai with such a low stipend spent money as I did. And how I blustered and swaggered about, with a trail of followers at my beck and call!

I wore kimonos of imported silk and fine fabrics that were beyond the reach of most people. I ate my fill of good food, and all my life I bought as many prostitutes as I liked. I lived life fully. Only recently have I come to my senses and begun to act more like a human being. When I think of my past, my hair stands on end.

He who would call himself a man would do well not to imitate my ways.

Any grandchildren or great grandchildren that I may have—let them read carefully what I have set down and take it as a warning. Even putting these words on paper fills me with shame.

I have no learning to speak of, having taught myself to write only in my twenties—and barely enough to cover my own needs at that. My friends were all bad and none good. Unable to distinguish right from wrong, I took my excesses as the behavior of heroes and brave men. In everything I was misguided, and I will never know how much anguish I caused my relatives, parents, wife, and children. Even more reprehensible, I behaved most disloyally to my lord and master the shogun and with uttermost defiance to my superiors. Thus did I finally bring myself to this low estate.

I am most fortunate in having a filial and obedient son. My daughters, too, are very devoted. My wife has never gone against my wishes. I am altogether satisfied to have lived until now without any serious mishap. At forty-two I have understood for the first time what it means to follow in the path of righteousness, to serve one's lord and one's father, to live with one's kinsmen in harmony, and to have compassion and love for one's wife, children, and servants.

My past conduct truly fills me with horror. Let my children, their children, and their children's children read this record carefully and savor its meaning. So be it.

Early winter, Tenpō 14, The Year of the Tiger*
Written at Uguisudani

*1843.

# NOTES TO THE TRANSLATION

1. Boy's Day, also called the Iris Festival, was observed on the fifth day of the fifth month. Sheaves of irises were hung from the eaves in the belief that the pungent odor would ward off evil spirits. In the game that Katsu refers to, known as *shōbu-uchi* or *shōbu-tataki*, plaited iris leaves are slapped against the ground to see whose last the longest, make the loudest noise, and so forth.

2. *Daikan*; as the head officer of a district within the shogunal domain (*tenryō*), the *daikan* governed an area with an assessed productivity from 50,000 to 100,000 *koku* and was responsible for taxes, public works, and judicial matters. He maintained residences in both Edo and the district. The retainers of nonsamurai rank mentioned in the text were called *chūgen*, literally, "in-between." Above commoners but below samurai, they were not allowed to bear surnames or swords. For performing menial tasks like guarding the gates, cleaning the house, and splitting firewood, they received about two *ryō* a year as well as room and board.

3. At the coming of age ceremony for sons of samurai, the hair at the front and on top of the head was shaved, and

the hair at the back and at the sides was gathered into a topknot. Katsu gave his age as seventeen because the shogunate did not allow the adoption of a male heir who was younger.

4. *Hanmoto mitodoke* or *hanmoto aratame*; procedure to ascertain such facts as the nature of the deceased's illness and the authenticity of the family seal when an urgent request was made to adopt a male heir into a samurai family. Ordinarily an heir had to be adopted before the death of the family head, but in *kobushin* families with a low rank-stipend, posthumous adoption was allowed and a near relative asked to stand in for the deceased.

5. *Hyaku monogatari*, literally, "one hundred tales." Participants told ghost stories in the dark by the light of candles. A candle was snuffed out at the end of each story, and it was thought that when the last candle went out, a ghost appeared.

6. As in other fields of art there was a tradition of secret transmission of techniques in swordsmanship. The exact nature of the stance called the *sō* is unclear, but it probably represented an elementary level of prowess.

7. *Tegata* or *sekisho tegata*; identification papers for passing through a barrier station. The papers set forth the bearer's name, address, purpose of travel, and other pertinent information. There were several barrier stations on the Tōkaidō, the coastal highway connecting Edo and Kyoto. The barrier station at Hakone was particularly stringent because of its proximity to Edo. Rules were generally relaxed for traveling entertainers, sumo wrestlers, and the like. See the map of Japan for the route of the Tōkaidō.

8. *Goma no hai* can also be interpreted as "ashes from a sacred fire," from the fact that many highway thieves disguised themselves as priests from Kōyasan, the Shingon Buddhist religious complex in Wakayama, and fobbed off

ashes with purportedly magic properties to unwary travelers. Even during the peaceful Tokugawa period, the highways were infested with thieves, tricksters, beggars, and prostitutes. Travelers were constantly warned to keep an eye on their luggage, to go to bed fully clothed, and so on.

9. Throughout the Tokugawa period pilgrimages to Ise Shrine were immensely popular. Located in Ise, formerly Uji-Yamada, on the Kii Peninsula, the shrine was dedicated to Amaterasu, the ancestral goddess of the imperial family. Pilgrimages were undertaken more for pleasure than for religious purposes, however, and it was not unusual for young boys and girls to go without permission from parents or employer. On these jaunts, called *nukemairi*, or "slipping-away pilgrimages," they often carried only a ladle and depended on charity for food and lodging.

10. Clerics of low rank called *onshi* or *oshi* were charged with providing food and lodging for pilgrims. They also traveled through the country proselytizing and raising funds for their institutions.

11. "Moto no Mokuami"; a phrase originating from a seventeenth-century chapbook, *Moto no Mokuami*, in which the eponymous hero Mokuami becomes a rich merchant only to discover that it was all a dream. According to another explanation, the phrase derives from the fact that when the gold leaf peels off a statue of the Amida Buddha, the statue becomes nothing more than an ordinary piece of wood.

12. *Yoriki*; middle- or low-ranking samurai who assisted the town magistrate as senior policemen. Numbering about twenty-five, they worked together with lesser policemen called *dōshin*. Besides in Edo, town magistrates were established in Osaka, Kyoto, and other cities under direct shogunate control. The post station of Fuchū was also known as Sunpu.

13. Jizō (Sanskrit: Ksitigarbha) was a Buddhist deity popularly regarded as the guardian of travelers, children, and

pregnant women. Another deity frequently enshrined in roadside shrines was Kannon (Sanskrit: Avolokitesvara), the Buddhist goddess of mercy.

14. Konpira or Kotohira Shrine, in what is now Kagawa Prefecture, was almost as popular as Ise. Now dedicated to the god Ōmononushi no mikoto and the Emperor Sutoku, it was originally dedicated to Konpira Daigongen, a deity believed to be derived from Kumbhira, the Indian crocodile god of the Ganges. Because of its proximity to the sea, the shrine was particularly popular with fishermen and sailors.

15. Also known as *urabon* (believed to be derived from the Sanskrit Ullambana); the Buddhist festival for the dead. It is observed on July fifteenth (in some areas, in August) with offerings of food, flowers, and lighted candles in the belief that the spirits of ancestors return to earth.

16. *Sando hikyaku*, literally, "three-times flying feet"; a courier in the employ of merchant houses that ran a thrice-monthly mail service between Edo and Kyoto/Osaka. It took an average of six days to cover the distance of about 280 miles, although a relay team of couriers was known to deliver the mail in sixty-eight hours.

17. Suzugamori, together with Kozukappara in Senju, was the site of a shogunate prison and execution grounds.

18. The discontinuation of a samurai's lineage (*zekke* or *kaieki*) was a particularly severe punishment for habitual drinking or gambling, administrative incompetence, or immoral conduct.

19. *Kurayado* were merchants at the shogunate warehouse in Asakusa who handled rice stipends for vassals. They also lent money to samurai on the security of their stipends and by one subterfuge or another usually charged more than the officially permitted rate of 15 percent a year.

20. Fairs were held throughout the year at the Sensōji temple in Asakusa. At the end-of-the-year fair (*toshi no ichi*),

pine decorations and other wares for the New Year were sold.

21. Several methods existed for determining a village's taxes. The most common within the shogun's domain was to take an average from the harvest of several previous years (*jōmen*). Another method was to estimate the yield visually or to take a sample cutting (*kemi* or *kenmi*). The official tax rate ranged from 40 to 60 percent, though only rarely was that much of the harvest actually collected in taxes. In this instance the village tax based on half of the yield of the poorest land meant an actual rate closer to 20 or 25 percent for the village as a whole. Since the average real tax rate was about 35 percent, the peasants had reason to be pleased.

22. Below the traditional classes of samurai, peasants, craftsmen, and tradesmen, there was a stratum of outcastes known as *eta*. These outcastes were ostracized by the rest of society and performed such tasks as disposing of animal carcasses and tanning leather. In 1871 the new Meiji government removed all social distinctions due to birth. In theory outcastes became full-fledged members of society, and the term *eta* itself was eschewed, but prejudice against the group still lingers.

23. Until dissolved by the Tenpō reforms (1838–1840), owners of public bathhouses in Edo were organized into a *kabunakama*, or monopoly guild. There was one stock (*kabu*) per establishment, each costing from three hundred to five hundred *ryō*, though some were worth as much as one thousand. A shareholder could own several establishments and either operate them himself or rent out his share on a monthly basis. At the time of the Tenpō reforms there were 570 bathhouses in the city.

24. Katsu says that he went to Suibara when he was eighteen, which would be 1819 (Bunsei 2). According to the *Dai Nihon jinmei jiten* and the *Bukan*, however, his brother

Hikoshirō was appointed district administrator in Shinano in 1813 (Bunka 10) and assigned to Suibara, Echigo, in 1821 (Bunsei 4), when Katsu would have been twenty.

25. The school was run by Katsu's second cousin Otani Seiichirō Nobutomo (1798–1864), who appears in the first half of the autobiography as Otani Shintarō. In 1817 Shintarō was adopted by Katsu's half brother Otani Hikoshirō, who had no son, and renamed Seiichirō. Soon after, he opened a school for fencing. He held a series of middle-level posts and in 1855 was appointed a commissioner of the Kōbusho, the newly established school for the military arts. To avoid confusion, he is referred to as Shintarō throughout the translation.

26. It is not clear what happened to the Katsu family property. Direct retainers of the shogun were given a house and plot of land (*hairyō yashiki*) proportionate to their rank-stipend. They were forbidden either to rent or sell their property. Like other impoverished samurai, Katsu probably rented out his property.

27. Mito was one of the three highest-ranking collateral houses of the Tokugawa family. "Harima-no-kami" is most probably a title that Katsu thought up to intimidate the post station officials.

28. Because of its changeable course and strategic position, the shogunate forbade the construction of a bridge over the Ōi River. One could ford the river on one's own, hire a coolie, or travel in style like Katsu on a litter (*rendai*). Rates rose with the water level, and when coolies began charging ninety-six copper pennies, it was generally considered too risky to cross on one's own.

29. Marishiten (Sanskrit: Marici); a Buddhist deity who was originally an attendant goddess to the sun. In Japan she became the patroness of samurai, who believed she made them impervious to danger.

30. *Kō*; a religious or fraternal association formed around

a shrine or temple to hold lectures, to go on pilgrimages, and for other edifying purposes. *Kō* were later formed to serve as savings or mutual help organizations. Members paid dues and took turns drawing from the common pool. When funds ran out, the association was usually dissolved. The Day of the Boar refers to a day in the traditional Japanese calendar in which the days of the month, as well as the year itself, were named after the signs of the ancient Chinese zodiac.

31. Myōken, also known as Hokushin Bosatsu, was believed to be a deification of Ursa Major. The Buddhist goddess was particularly favored by members of the *kobushingumi*.

32. Ryōbu Shingon, literally, "Two Aspects Mantra"; an esoteric school of Buddhism introduced to Japan by Kūkai in the ninth century. Believers were taught to seek enlightenment through the contemplation of two sacred drawings, one depicting the cosmic Buddha in his aspect as unchanging and indestructible, and the other in his aspect as immanent in all things. Shingon Buddhism also emphasized secret rites involving certain gestures and postures, the handling of implements, and the recitation of mantras, or mystical formulae. In its popular form these practices were used to invoke supernatural help in everyday life. It is not clear whether Tonomura was a priest or merely conversant with such arcana.

33. It was commonly believed that one could be possessed by the spirit of a dead person (*shiryō*), particularly by someone who had died an unnatural death, or by the spirit of a living person (*ikiryō*), such as a jealous rival in love.

34. Originally a deity of cereals, Inari Daimyōjin came to be associated with material prosperity and was popular with samurai, merchants, and craftsmen alike. Inari was usually represented by his messenger, a white fox.

35. *Kagetomi*; literally, "shadow lottery." An illegal lottery

that gave cash prizes on the numbers drawn at official lotteries. Although the shogunate forbade lotteries and other forms of gambling, it permitted certain religious institutions in Edo—the Yushima Tenjin, Meguro Fudō, and Kannōji in Yanaka—to hold lotteries to raise money for repairs.

36. Samurai were allowed to test their new swords on the corpses of criminals who had been executed. They also tested their skills and weapons by decapitating corpses that were placed on specially constructed earthen mounds. Asauemon is Yamada Asauemon, the official executioner of the shogunate. The name and post were hereditary.

37. Through a relative who was a lady-in-waiting at Edo Castle, Rintarō had become a companion *(koshō)* to Hatsunojō, the young grandson of the then shogun, Tokugawa Ienari. Hatsunojō (later Yoshimasa) succeeded to the Hitotsubashi branch of the Tokugawa family in 1837 but died the following year.

38. *Kojūningumi*; a unit of escort guards for the shogun when he left the castle. Katsu's account of Yamaguchi, who was appointed district administrator of Ichikawa, Kōshū, is corroborated by Murakami Tadashi in his *Tenryō* (Tokyo, 1965). In 1837, the year after peasants in the area had rioted over a shortage of food due to a series of bad harvest, Hayama Magosaburō was accused of taking money set aside for peasant relief and lending it to the peasants at usurious rates. Yamaguchi was unable to control the angry peasants, and recalled to Edo, was demoted the following year. It should be noted that assignment to far-off Kōshū was generally considered undesirable.

39. According to the *Tokushi biyō*, Makino Nagato-no-kami Shigefumi was appointed magistrate of Nagasaki in 1829 (Bunsei 12), and Kuze Ise-no-kami Hiromasa in 1833 (Tenpō 4). Rintarō was bitten by a dog in 1831, so this incident must have taken place earlier.

40. Katsu writes in the *kana* script *kafu mono*, meaning "something to buy." He surely means the opposite, or as Mr. Kawaguchi Hiroshi, the annotator of the Chūō kōron sha edition, suggests, he may have meant *kabusemono*, a fake.

41. *Kitsune bakuchi*, literally, "fox gambling." When a player shook three dice with the same number, he got back four times the original bet.

42. Shimada Toranosuke Kenzan (1810–1864); a samurai from the Nakatsu domain in Buzen Province. He later taught fencing to Rintarō and also acted as his mentor, advising him to practice Zen-like spiritual discipline. According to some accounts, it was on Toranosuke's suggestion that Rintarō took up Western studies—a decision that later proved crucial to his rapid rise in the shogunate bureaucracy.

43. Katsu writes *funyū* in the *kana* script. It is not clear whether he means the peasants' right to deny entry to shogunate officials, or whether, as Professor Katsube Mitake has recently suggested, he means *funyō*, meaning "prosperous" or "well-off."

44. Shimaya was one of several merchant houses that conducted a mail service between Edo and Osaka. It was not unusual for bannermen to borrow from their fiefs, but the peasants in Goganzuka seem to have been especially docile. According to Abe Yoshio ("Bushi no kōshi no seikatsu," Shinji Yoshimoto ed., *Edo jidai bushi no seikatsu*), when one bannerman with a rank-stipend of 1,250 *koku* tried to borrow money from his fiefs in the 1820s, he was not only refused but told to retrench by 50 percent. The peasants, moreover, spelled out the particulars, demanding that he spend 12 *ryō* for clothes rather than 22, one and a half *bu* for pocket money rather than two *bu*, and so on.

45. The reader may wonder from time to time whether Katsu was entirely truthful in his somewhat boastful accounts of his exploits. In this instance, at least, his account has been

largely corroborated by documents recently discovered on one of the old Okano fiefs near Tokyo by Professor Ōguchi Yūjirō of Ochanomizu University. The documents make clear that the Okano family was indeed in straitened financial condition at the time of the event. Furthermore, an 1839 letter written by a village official of Goganzuka states that Katsu had visited the village the previous year and that the villagers extracted an agreement from Katsu that in the future they would advance loans only if they received a formal written order from Magoichirō. The article containing this information is "Musui dokugen no kyozō to jitsuzō," in *Edo to wa nani ka: Edo no bakumatsu*, 1986. I am grateful to Professor Tamai Kensuke for calling it to my attention. It has been translated as "The Reality Behind *Musui Dokugen*: The World of the *Hatamoto* and *Gokenin*," *Journal of Japanese Studies* 16 (Summer 1990): 289–308.

46. The five major festivals designated by the shogunate were Jinjitsu (first day of the first month), Jōshi (third day of the third month), Tango (fifth day of the fifth month), Shichiseki (seventh day of the seventh month), and Chōyō (ninth day of the ninth month). Debts were orginarily paid just before the Bon festival and at the end of the year, but in some parts of Japan payment was made on these feast days as well.

# APPENDIX ONE
*Genealogy of Katsu Kokichi*

According to one account of the Otani family's origins, Heizō's father, blind from birth, had gone as a youth from a village in Echigo (now Niigata Prefecture) to try his luck in Edo. He built a fortune as a moneylender—an occupation open to the blind—and bought his way up to the highest rank in the blindmen's guild. He then attained respectability by having his third son, Heizō, adopted as the heir of the Otani. Known in his later years as Yoneyama Kengyō, he probably died a contented man, for according to the same account, on his deathbed he burnt all the notes for his outstanding loans and left to his nine children seventeen plots of land in Edo and 300,000 gold pieces.

The lineage of the Katsu family was more distinguished. According to the *Kansei Revised Samurai Genealogies*, an ancestor, Katsu Tokinao, served Tokugawa Ieyasu in Mikawa before the hegemon unified Japan in 1600. Tokinao's great great-grandson Nobumasa was made Captain of the Inner Guard (*ohiroshikiban*) with a rank-stipend of four hundred *koku*, and his son Tomomichi was made a member of the

Great Guard (*ōgoban*) in 1776, with a stipend of two hundred *koku*. Tomomichi had no son, and in 1783 he adopted his sister's child, Aoki Motoyoshi—Katsu's adoptive father. All of Katsu's immediate ancestors are listed as having had the privilege of audience with the shogun.

*Otani Family*

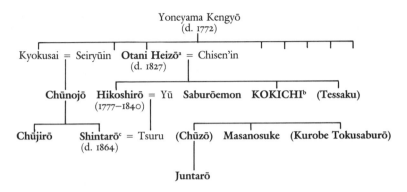

*Katsu Family*

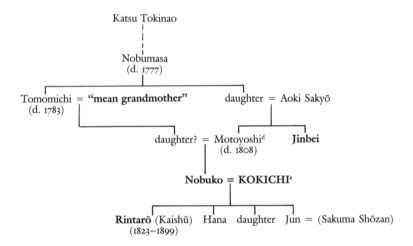

NOTE: Names mentioned in the text are shown in boldface type; names enclosed in parentheses indicate those not in the official genealogy.

[a] Adopted by the Otani family.

[b] Child of a concubine.

[c] Child of a concubine; adopted by Hikoshirō and renamed Seiichirō.

[d] Adopted by Tomomichi.

[e] Adopted by Motoyoshi.

# APPENDIX TWO
*Currency in the Tokugawa Period*

Gold was the basis for currency in Edo. The standard unit was 1 *ryō* (18 grams).

1 *ryō* = 4 *bu* = 16 *shu*

Silver was the basis in the Kyoto-Osaka region. The standard unit was 1 *monme* (3.76 grams).

1 *monme* = 10 *fun* = 100 *rin*
1,000 *monme* = 1 silver *kan* or *kanme*
60 *monme* = 1 *ryō*

Copper currency was used throughout the country. Copper coins had square holes in the center and were strung together with a strand of hemp in groups of 100 (actually 96) and 1,000 (actually 960) *mon*.

1,000 *mon* = 1 copper *kan*
4,000 *mon* = 60 *monme* = 1 *ryō*

The exchange rate between gold and silver remained fairly stable through the Tokugawa period, but copper was steadily devalued. By the 1830s and 1840s, 1 *ryō* equaled about 6,500 copper *mon*.

In 1805 (Bunka 2) one could buy a decent lunch of mushrooms, pickles, rice, and soup for 100 copper *mon*. In 1825 (Bunsei 8), when 1 *koku* of rice sold for about 63 silver *monme* on the market, the price of 1 *shō* (1 *shō* = 1.8 liter) of salt was 32 *mon*; ten *daikon*, or radish, 258 *mon*; ten peaches 15 *mon*; ten pears 70 *mon*; six apples 32 *mon*; and a bunch of carrots 5 *mon*. In 1830 (Tenpō 1), when 1 *koku* of rice fetched about the same price, 1 *shō* of soy sauce was 110 *mon*. In 1835 (Tenpō 6) one could buy a piece of wool cloth measuring 1½ yards by 2 yards for 395 *monme*, or 6½ *ryō*. A grown-up could go to the public bath for 8 *mon* and a child for 5 *mon*. A carpenter could earn 420 to 450 *mon* a day, then considered a decent wage. By 1866 (Keiō 2), when 7,000 *mon* equaled 1 *ryō*, a hairdresser cost 64 *mon*, a visit to the bathhouse 16 *mon*, one cucumber 16 to 20 *mon*, and one eggplant 12 *mon*.

# BIBLIOGRAPHY

Etō Jun, ed. *Katsu Kaishū* Nihon no meicho series, vol. 32. Chūō kōron sha, 1984.

Hayashi Jussai, comp. *Kansei chōshū shokafu.* Zokugunsho ruijū kanseikai, 1964–66 reprint.

Inagaki Shisei. *Buke jiten.* Seiabō, 1958.

———. *Edo seikatsu jiten.* Seiabō, 1963.

———. *Kōshō buke no sekai.* Kōsōsha, 1978.

Katsube Mitake, ed. *Katsu Kokichi: Musui dokugen.* Tōyō bunko series, no. 138. Heibonsha, 1969.

Matsudaira Tarō. *Edo jidai seido no kenkyū.* Reprint. Kashiwa shobō, 1964.

Matsuura Rei. *Katsu Kaishū.* Chūō kōron sha, 1968.

Mitamura Engyo. *Buke no seikatsu.* Seiabō, 1959.

Miyamoto Mataji et. al. *Kinsei Ōsaka no bukka to rishi.* Sōbunsha, 1963.

Murakami Tadashi. *Tenryō.* Jinbutsu ōraisha, 1964.

Nanjō Norio. *Kōshō Edo jiten.* Jinbutsu ōraisha, 1965.

Nishimura Matsunosuke and Haga Noboru, eds. *Edo sanbyakunen.* Kōdansha, 1975–76.

Ōguchi Yūjirō. "Musui dokugen no kyozō to jitsuzō." In

*Edo to wa nani ka: Edo no bakumatsu*, edited by Katsu-be Mitake and Inoue Isao. Shibundō, 1986. Translated as "The Reality Behind *Musui Dokugen*: The World of the *Hatamoto* and *Gokenin*," *Journal of Japanese Studies* 16 (Summer 1990): 289–308.

Osatake Takeki. *Tobaku to suri no kenkyū*. Jitsugyō no Nihonsha, 1948.

Sasama Yoshihiko. *Edo bakufu yakushoku shūsei*. Yūzan-kaku, 1965.

Shinji Yoshimoto. *Edo jidai no buke no seikatsu*. Shibundō, 1961.

————, ed. *Edo jidai bushi no seikatsu*. Yūzankaku, 1962.

Shinmi Kichiji. *Hatamoto*. Yoshikawa kōbunkan, 1967.

Takai Ranzan. *O-Edo ōezu*. 1859.

Takayanagi Kaneyoshi. *Edo jidai gokenin no seikatsu*. Yūzankaku, 1963.

Tamura Eitarō. *Katsu Rintarō*. Yūzankaku, 1967.

Totman, Conrad. *Politics in the Tokugawa Bakufu* 1600–1843. Cambridge: Harvard University Press, 1967.

Watanabe Ichirō, comp. *Tokugawa bakufu daimyō hata-moto yakushoku bukan*. Kashiwa shobō, 1967.

Yamamura, Kozo. *A Study of Samurai Income and Entre-preneurship*. Cambridge: Harvard University Press, 1974.

*Tokushi biyō*. Tokyo daigaku shiryō hensanjo, 1935.